C000055900

SMOOTHLY FROM HARROW

SMOOTHLY FROM HARROW

A COMPENDIUM FOR
THE LONDON COMMUTER

BY CHRIS MOSS

Published by Blue Guides Limited,
a Somerset Books Company
Winchester House, Deane Gate Avenue,
Taunton, Somerset TA1 2UH.
www.blueguides.com
"Blue Guide" is a registered trademark.

ISBN 978–1–905131–62–4

A CIP catalogue record of this book is available from the
British Library.

Pre-press by Anikó Kuzmich and Hadley Kincade
Printed in Hungary by Dürer Nyomda Kft., Gyula.

CONTENTS

For Bob Greig, formerly of Paddington Station, and
anyone arriving in London for the very first time

PREFACE

In my beginning is my end

The London commuter gets far less attention than he deserves. For a start, he is legion. Some 860,000 people arrive in London by train every day and another 400,000 travel to work on the Tube. Some 7,500 buses carry six million passengers every weekday, and then there are the walkers, motorcyclists, drivers and the ever-increasing pelotons of urban cyclists. More than half a million trips are made by bike every day. Second, the commuter built London. Look at maps from 1800, 1850, 1900 and today and you will see how a city that used to peter out into fields around Marble Arch in the west and Bethnal Green in the east spread its limbs out along the suburban railway lines that were built from the 1830s. But the commuter is not just a number nor merely a load for these lines; he is the key witness of all that passes in the capital and its environs. During a single journey to work, a commuter will see – and be seen by – thousands of people. Thousands more on the way home. Yet, for all that, he so often seems invisible, cast aside. The trainspotters and other siderodromologists have ensured that modes of transport receive an excess of attention. The ties between the chattering/scribbling classes and what is imagined as the "real" city – Zones 1 and 2, Soho, Clerkenwell, middle-class Hackney, art galleries and retail spaces, offices, bars – keep the cityscape prominent. The suburbs, too, have produced a Babel of a library across all media, filled with poetry, derision, self-mockery. The commuter, though long imagined as a ghost-figure who is either on the platform out of town waiting or, suddenly, skipping fast down the street in the centre, aimed for work, is in fact the connection between these worlds. He – and she – is not only a face in the crowd, but an individual, too.

Smoothly from Harrow is a collection of confessions, including my own confession of failing to be a commuter, a Londoner, a reliable worker. It is a compendium of thoughts and images and ideas that derive from the commuter and his milieux: home, platform, seat, workplace. Between the lofty and literary references are some lighter facts and lyrics, perhaps to while away a delayed ride to work. If you have ever been a commuter or indeed are currently performing that role, this little book, part-manual, part-homage, is dedicated to you ■

Chris Moss, Laugharne (via Harrow and Surbiton), Autumn 2013

1

ORIGIN

"You do look nice, Lupin."

Lupin replied: "Yes, it's a good make-up, isn't it?

A regular-downright-respectable-funereal-

first-class-City-firm-junior-clerk."

He laughed rather ironically.

In January 1988, when I was 21, I decided to slough off the trappings of freedom, studenthood, youth, promise and coolness – and become a commuter. I relocated to Harrow on the Hill, where two friends who were renting a maisonette had a spare room. I'd recently finished a degree in theology, so was essentially unemployable. Like quite a few other directionless jobseekers in the late 1980s I decided to become a chartered accountant. Looking back, this now seems hilariously improbable, but I was naïve, broke, prone to self-immolation, and the established, ever-expanding, firm in Blackfriars was open to unskilled graduates. Harrow fitted my new project. Previously I'd loitered around Camden, Westminster, Manor House, Tooting. I was leaving grit behind. Harrow, with its posh school and wide boulevards appeared to provide a future, of sorts.

I bought an off-the-peg suit, a blue-black Crombie coat, five shirts and five ties, shiny black shoes and a leather-handled brolly. My mum, to congratulate me on my new respectability, bought me some black leather gloves with red silk lining. I purchased a briefcase, but a schoolmaster-type brown affair, to show that if I was going to do the stereotype thing, I was going to do it my way.

The journey in, on the shambolically fast Metropolitan line, was thrilling for the first fortnight. I would stand – there were rarely empty seats – and look out on Wembley, Willesden, Finchley. Once in London I tried several routes to the office, but in the end opted to go all the way round through Aldgate. I didn't think too much about it at the time, but I had started my working life on the railway line that had opened up the suburbs that came to be known as Metroland and on the world's oldest underground line.

It was a performance. I liked TS Eliot's *The Waste Land* and those seductive lines: "A crowd flowed over London Bridge, so many, I had not thought death had undone so many." I felt as if I was on the way to becoming a hollow man and that seemed desirable. I invented some spurious connection between the travelling undead of the morning and the existential anti-heroes

"Zone One has become a theme park, a branded mews. The suburbs surely must reclaim their rightful place..."

of the fiction of Max Frisch, Camus and Sartre. I tricked myself, told myself stories. "For the most banal even to become an adventure," writes Roland Barthes, "you must (and this is enough) begin to recount it."

And then the calamity. In my third week into the job – which seemed to consist mainly in adding long columns of numbers, surprisingly enough – I found myself feeling withdrawn and yet watchful in the mornings, leaning up against the long window of the carriage door, looking out more and more on the parks and open spaces, and eyeing the sunrise. The journey home, through the dark evenings of late winter, seemed endless. I gave up the job, and the commute, and the gloves.

Far away from commuterland now, I remain what Barthes would have derided as a "minor hysteric", taking pleasure in, and feeling curiosity about, the commuting life. When I focus on the mundanity of the commute – the morning drizzle, the mournful waiting, the grey faces – I am indulging a fancy, enjoying

the "hallucinatory relish of 'reality'". I am also thinking about myself, about some commuter trapped inside me, the life I didn't get around to living.

But London is a strange city now, a city of strangers. Its centre is a residential ghetto for Qatari despots, Russian oligarchs and Greek billionaires – or at least their exiled money. The urban snobbery of the liberal commentariat seems more misplaced than ever. Zone One has become a theme park, a branded mews. The suburbs surely must reclaim their rightful place, aligning themeslves with the inner and the outer city: Hackney and Haslemere, Watford and White City; they have the commuter in common.

During the writing and compiling of this book I revisited some familiar commutes. This was fradulent, I admit. I was not on my way to work, or rather, I was not on my way to a regimented office space or a factory or a shop. I was on my way to a library, to search for thoughts, texts, numbers, lists, pictures, more successful commuters than myself – in fact and fiction. Here are some of my favourites ∎

Etymologies
Commute/Commuting/Commuter/Commutation

Latin root, *commutare*: to often change, or change entirely, from *com* – the intensive/intensifying prefix – + *mutare* to change.

1633. To exchange/change into: "From time to time, exchange and commute, as well Moneys currant of England, into Moneys of this new Standerd of Ireland."
Pacata Hibernia

1844. Reduce a sentence: "The [capital] sentence was commuted to imprisonment for life."
Horace Hayman Wilson, *History of British India from 1805 to 1835 (1844–48)*

1848. Commutation ticket: Transportation ticket sold for a fixed number of trips over the same route during a limited period. *American Railway Journal*

1865. Railway, or rather, railroad line: "Two or three may be styled commuters' roads, running chiefly for the accommodation of city business-men with suburban residences." *Atlantic Monthly*

1889. Passenger: "Commuter, one who commutes."
Century Dictionary

1906. Season-ticket passenger: "There are many business men who practically divide their time between New York and Chicago, and 'commute' (the American term for taking season tickets)."
Daily Chronicle

1932. Still obscure in the UK: "Many things familiar in America need explaining in Britain: *'commuters' zone'.*" *Times Literary Supplement*

1962. London commuter established as a type:
"The people who are 'something in the City' to-day mostly commute to Sussex and Surrey." *Daily Telegraph*

How many miles to Babylon?

How many miles to Babylon?
Three-score miles and ten.
Can I get there by candle-light?
Yes, there and back again.
If your heels are nimble and light,
You will get there by candle-light.

Trad. (early nineteenth century)

The commuters' social hierarchy

Alpha: Rail User
Literary, reflective, suburban or semi-suburban,
iconic, time-honoured.

Beta: Tube User
Semi-literary, stoical, lives in the dark,
blind to the journey.

Gamma: Walker
Urban, green, genteel, classical, lucky.

Delta: Cyclist
Fashionable, fit, proud, the future,
self-satisfied, sweaty.

Epsilon: Bus User
Time-honoured, long-suffering, bullied
by bad brakes, baked by cruel heating;
waiting for Godot, every day.

Omega: Car Driver
Trapped, can't talk, can't eat an apple, can't
read a book, viewed with contempt, or envy.
The past.

Charles Dickens on the coming of the railroad

The first shock of a great earthquake had, just at that period, rent the whole neighbourhood to its centre. Traces of its course were visible on every side. Houses were knocked down; streets broken through and stopped; deep pits and trenches dug in the ground; enormous heaps of earth and clay thrown up; buildings that were undermined and shaking, propped by great beams of wood. Here, a chaos of carts, overthrown and jumbled together, lay topsy-turvy at the bottom of a steep unnatural hill; there, confused treasures of iron soaked and rusted in something that had accidentally become a pond. Everywhere were bridges that led nowhere; thoroughfares that were wholly impassable; Babel towers of chimneys, wanting half their height; temporary wooden houses and enclosures, in the most unlikely situations; carcasses of ragged tenements, and fragments of unfinished walls and arches, and piles of scaffolding, and wildernesses of bricks, and giant forms of cranes, and tripods straddling above nothing. There were a hundred thousand shapes and substances of incompleteness, wildly mingled out of their places, upside down, burrowing in the earth, aspiring in the air, mouldering in the water, and unintelligible as any dream. Hot springs and fiery eruptions, the usual attendants upon earthquakes, lent their contributions of confusion to the scene. Boiling water hissed and heaved within dilapidated walls; whence, also, the glare and roar of flames came issuing forth; and mounds of ashes blocked up rights of way, and wholly changed the law and custom of the neighbourhood. In short, the yet unfinished and unopened Railroad was in progress; and, from the very core of all this dire disorder, trailed smoothly away, upon its mighty course of civilisation and improvement.

From Dombey and Son *(1848)*

Tiresias (aka Roger Green)

The commuter – *l'homme moyen de notre*
époque. The anti-hero of our age. More
than the soldier, the nuclear physicist,
the political prisoner or the starving child,
he indicates where we've gone wrong.

From Notes from Overground *(1984)*

Populations

Figures taken from the 2011 Census

10 MOST DENSELY POPULATED LONDON BOROUGHS

Croydon 363,000
Barnet 356,000
Ealing 338,000
Enfield 313,000
Brent 311,000
Bromley 309,000
Newham 308,000
Wandsworth 307,000
Lambeth 303,000
Southwark 288,000

SOUTH EAST ENGLAND
8.6 million
LONDON 8.2 million

10 MOST DENSELY POPULATED COMMUTER TOWNS/AREAS

Brighton and Hove 273,000
Medway 264,000
Milton Keynes 249,000
Southampton 237,000
Portsmouth 205,000
New Forest 177,000
Aylesbury Vale 174,000
Wycombe 172,000
Basingstoke and Deane 168,000
Reading 156,000

THE CITY OF LONDON
Resident population 7,375
Working population 350,000

Natural havens on the railways

As people commute, buried in headphones and newspapers, they ignore what they probably see as no-man's land, areas of scrub or neglect, places that seem separate from themselves and their lives. How wrong this impression is: the verges that run for miles along our transportation routes are vital areas of escape for some of the countryside's main players, from small and often unnoticed species right through to the royalty of the UK's tree population. The areas beside the tracks provide welcome space for plants and animals to thrive.

Often disturbed and worked over, railway verges are suited to the plant pioneers who set the pace for succession and the longer-term build-up of nature. There is no better example of this than the nettle (*Urtica diocia*), a plant feared by children and often despised by adults. In fact our spiky friends are a vital source of food for the larvae of butterflies such as the Peacock and countless moths such as the sinister-sounding Gothic. Nettles are rich in nitrogen and this, at the end of each growing season, replenishes the soil and enables other species to move in. One beneficiary in late spring is the common primrose (*Primula vulgaris*), which thrives near railway tracks, its seed dispersal aided by the slipstreams of trains, its beautiful, pale yellow flowers bringing a smile to any observant passenger. Many plain-looking plants also seek refuge in the railways' green corridors. The red fescue (*Festuca rubra*), though originating overseas, has gone native and helps form a sward that guards against erosion and provides cover for numerous insects, including the lively Azure Damselfly.

Some familiar favourites will always be present on the railway sides. The common bramble (*Rubus fruticosa*) waits for its chance and moves in to conquer any ground that humans dare to rearrange. It may not be the prettiest of plants but it provides cover for the bigger mammals such as foxes. It also plays a vital role in the most important act of nature, paving the way for succession: it is pivotal in the build-up of soil on which bigger species can then take hold, such as birch (*Betula pendula*) and field maple (*Acer campestre*). These form the beginnings of the ultimate eco-system: the woodland.

Our often unnoticed railway verges are important centres for wildlife development and havens for trees, and if they're allowed to flourish they will also help check aggressive non-native plants such as Japanese knotweed (*Fallopia japonica*). So next time you're squashed on a train at rush hour, take a moment to gaze out of the window and spare a smile for the nature that is going about its business.

Chris M Collins,
Patron, Trees for Cities

First-class passengers

JOHN LE CARRÉ

When he was still David John Moore Cornwell and working for MI5 he wrote his first novel, *Call for the Dead* (1961) on the train from Great Missenden to Marylebone; his wife typed up his script every night. He came up with the name John Le Carré while riding a bus over Battersea Bridge.

HENRY VIII

After a fire destroyed his Westminster Palace in 1512, Henry relocated to Greenwich and spent almost two decades commuting up the Thames to London and also on to Richmond and to Cardinal Wolsey's home at Hampton Court, which he later incorporated into his property portfolio.

TS ELIOT

He commuted from his house in West Street, Marlow (Shelley and Mary Shelley once lived in the same street) in Buckinghamshire to his job in the Colonial and Foreign Department at Lloyds Bank. "The train journey is restful," he wrote to his mother in June 1918.

WALTER DE LA MARE

The poet, novelist and supernaturalist commuted for 18 years from Beckenham and, later, Anerley, to his accountancy job at the Anglo-American (Standard) Oil Company; his father, James Edward Delamaere, had commuted from Charlton to the Bank of England on a horse; his son Richard, connoisseur of East Asian porcelain and pioneer of organic farming, commuted to his job at Faber & Faber in Russell Square from Essex in an open-top Lagonda.

STANLEY SPENCER

Between 1908 and 1912 the artist commuted by train every day from the Thames-side village of Cookham, Berkshire – "a village in Heaven" in his opinion – to the Slade School of Art, then part of University College London.

JG BALLARD

Author of a number of novels set in London's suburbs, Ballard commuted for several years from homes in Chiswick, Twickenham and Shepperton, finally giving up his job of deputy editor at *Chemistry and Industry* magazine in Belgrave Square in 1963 to become a full-time writer.

DYLAN THOMAS

In his to-ings and fro-ings between the pubs and social hubs of Fitzrovia and his various rural hideouts in Laugharne and Newport in Wales, Thomas exemplified the classic town-and-country tension beloved of artists and writers: fun and excess in the city, poetry, peace and, in Thomas's case, a few more pints in the country.

CHARLES DICKENS

Began and ended his life with commutes and walked as much as 20 miles per day. As a child he walked the four miles from Camden to the Warren's Blacking Factory at Hungerford Market

on the Embankment. In his later years he travelled by train to Higham in Kent, close to his home at Gad's Hill; on at least one occasion he walked the 30 miles from central London to Gad's Hill (in *Great Expectations*, Pip undertakes a similar journey, albeit in the other direction).

MRS BEETON
By 1860, Isabella Beeton had progressed from translating French novels for serialisation in her husband, Sam's *Englishwoman's Domestic Magazine* to

editing it; she commuted in from Pinner every day with Sam – leaving her young child at home – in the otherwise all-male first-class carriage.

DR RICHARD BEECHING
Beeching (*pictured*) commuted from East Grinstead to London in the 1960s, when he was chairman of the British Railways Board. The street that honours his memory, Beeching Way – part of the A22 – was built on one of the two local railway lines that he closed; some locals wanted to call it Beeching Cut.

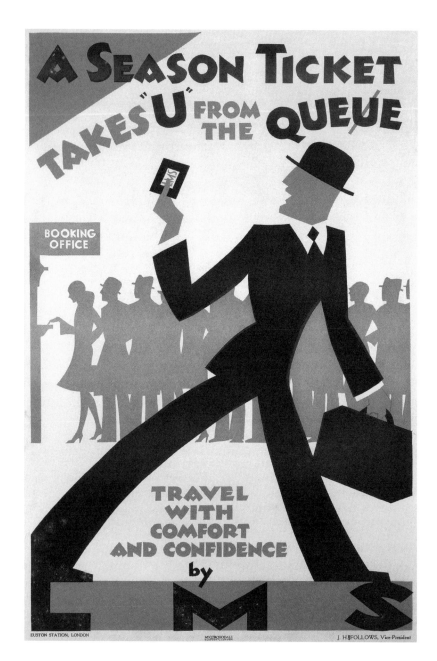

Lupin dresses for work

My great dream of the last few weeks – in fact, of many years – has been realised. This morning came a letter from Mr. Perkupp, asking me to take Lupin down to the office with me. I went to Lupin's room; poor fellow, he seemed very pale, and said he had a bad headache. He had come back yesterday from Gravesend, where he spent part of the day in a small boat on the water, having been mad enough to neglect to take his overcoat with him. I showed him Mr. Perkupp's letter, and he got up as quickly as possible. I begged of him not to put on his fast-coloured clothes and ties, but to dress in something black or quiet-looking. Carrie was all of a tremble when she read the letter, and all she could keep on saying was: "Oh, I do hope it will be all right." For myself, I could scarcely eat any breakfast. Lupin came down dressed quietly, and looking a perfect gentleman, except that his face was rather yellow. Carrie, by way of encouragement said: "You do look nice, Lupin." Lupin replied: "Yes, it's a good make-up, isn't it? A regular-downright-respectable-funereal-first-class-City-firm-junior-clerk." He laughed rather ironically.

From Diary of a Nobody *(1892) by George Grossmith and Weedon Grossmith*

Neil Gaiman goes underground

When he had first arrived, he had found London huge, fundamentally incomprehensible, with only the Tube map, that elegant multicoloured topographical display of underground railway lines and stations, giving it any semblance of order. Gradually he realised that the Tube map was a handy fiction that made life easier, but bore no resemblance to the reality of the shape of the city above: like belonging to a political party, he thought once, proudly, and then, having tried to explain the resemblance between the Tube map and politics, as a party, to a cluster of bewildered strangers, he had decided in the future to leave political comment to others.

From Neverwhere (1996)

THE CITY GENT: STRIPPED

1. THE BOWLER

"Between England and Revolution there will always be an army of bowler hats." Seán Ó Faoláin

Art critics dispute whether Magritte's favourite hat was a symbol of bland conformity and petit bourgeois attitudes or a semantically-layered signifier ripe for surrealist refinition. Bowler wearers in the 21st century are liable to be targets of less flattering critiquing, but their headgear has a cultural heritage that belies its fusty "chartered accountant" image.

In 1849, Edward Coke, the younger brother of the 2nd Earl of Leicester, asked hatters Lock & Co of St James's for a hat for his gamekeeper. He needed a smart but solid helmet to protect his pate from low-hanging branches when on horseback. London hatmakers Thomas and William Bowler were given the commission. When Coke arrived at the shop in London, he is said to have stamped on the crown twice to test its robustness. He paid 12 shillings for the new hat.

As was the custom in the trade, the hat was named a Coke after the client. But when the brothers started manufacturing 60,000 a year it became known as the bowler. Made from felt stiffened with Shellac, it combined a practical bowl-shaped crown and a slender

rim with a dash of elegance in the silk ribbon. Less formal than the top hat, traditionally worn by the upper classes, but more respectable than the soft felt hats used by the lower-middle classes, the bowlers were immediately popular not only with gamekeepers, but also with landowners, coach drivers and city workers. Soon the hat was adopted by market and street traders, shipyard workers and builders – for whom it was an early "hard hat" – as well as insurance agents and salesmen. A bye-law – still in force – required that horse-drawn Hackney cabs be built high enough to accommodate a man wearing a bowler hat.

The discreet but smart bowler hat became the defining feature among London's conservative City workforce. This lasted until the 1960s, when youth culture, central heating, long hair and car ownership conspired to make hats in general uncool and the bowler in particular a symbol of stiff, dated formality.

Culturally, however, the Bowler never went out of fashion. It was the hat of Winston Churchill and Stanley Baldwin, Charlie Chaplin and Laurel and Hardy. In Samuel Beckett's *Waiting for Godot*, the only specification for costume is that all four characters wear a bowler. It is worn by The Riddler in Batman, by Thomson and

Thompson in the Tintin books (surely an allusion to Magritte) and by Oddjob in the James Bond novels and films. In the 1970s, cartoon character Mister Benn never left 52 Festive Road without one, and Alex DeLarge in Stanley Kubrick's *A Clockwork Orange* (1971) has spawned a global cult of bowler-wearing punk-brat rebels (including the Windsor brothers).

In Milan Kundera's *The Unbearable Lightness of Being*, Tomas and Sabina are almost moved to tears while making love in the presence of a bowler hat that reminds them of their own past lovemaking and also of a pre-modern, better world. The bowler continues to add a dash of incongruous rakishness to the scalps of indigenous high-plains Bolivians.

"A Well Respected Man" (1965) – The Kinks

Cause he gets up in the morning,
And he goes to work at nine,
And he comes back home at five-thirty,
Gets the same train every time.
Cause his world is built round punctuality,
It never fails.

And he's oh, so good,
And he's oh, so fine,
And he's oh, so healthy,
In his body and his mind.
He's a well respected man about town,
Doing the best things so conservatively.

Sherlock Holmes and the commuter

"Some years ago – to be definite, in May, 1884 – there came to Lee a gentleman, Neville St. Clair by name, who appeared to have plenty of money. He took a large villa, laid out the grounds very nicely, and lived generally in good style. By degrees he made friends in the neighbourhood, and in 1887 he married the daughter of a local brewer, by whom he now has two children. He had no occupation, but was interested in several companies and went into town as a rule in the morning, returning by the 5:14 from Cannon Street every night. Mr. St. Clair is now thirty-seven years of age, is a man of temperate habits, a good husband, a very affectionate father, and a man who is popular with all who know him. I may add that his whole debts at the present moment, as far as we have been able to ascertain, amount to £88 10s., while he has £220 standing to his credit in the Capital and Counties Bank. There is no reason, therefore, to think that money troubles have been weighing upon his mind.

"Last Monday Mr. Neville St. Clair went into town rather earlier than usual, remarking before he started that he had two important commissions to perform, and that he would bring his little boy home a box of bricks. Now, by the merest chance, his wife received a telegram upon this same Monday, very shortly after his departure, to the effect that a small parcel of considerable value which she had been expecting was waiting for her at the offices of the Aberdeen Shipping Company. Now, if you are well up in your London, you will know that the office of the company is in Fresno Street, which branches out of Upper Swandam Lane, where you found me to-night. Mrs. St. Clair had her lunch, started for the City, did some shopping, proceeded to the company's office, got her packet, and found herself at exactly 4:35 walking through Swandam Lane on her way back to the station. Have you followed me so far?"

"It is very clear."

"If you remember, Monday was an exceedingly hot day, and Mrs. St. Clair walked slowly, glancing about in the hope of seeing a cab, as she did not like the neighbourhood in which she found herself. While she was walking in this way down Swandam Lane, she suddenly heard an ejaculation or cry, and was struck cold to see her husband looking down at her and, as it seemed to her, beckoning to her from a second-floor window. The window was open, and she distinctly saw his face, which she describes as being terribly agitated. He waved his hands frantically to her, and then vanished from the window so suddenly that it seemed to her that he had been plucked back by some irresistible force from behind. One singular point which struck her quick feminine eye was that although he wore some dark coat, such as he had started to town in, he had on neither collar nor necktie…

From The Man with the Twisted Lip *(1891) by Sir Arthur Conan Doyle*

Commuter Caricatures

SILLY WALKER
Strides at insane speed – he really,
really wants to run – across the
concourse of the terminal; M&S suit,
middle-management/age/class/riff;
married, late.

REBEL WITHOUT A TIE
Displays a self-consciously dishevelled,
possibly stubbly look; been doing the
Maidstone-Victoria run for years but still
can't quite believe it; aged 37 to 44, can't
believe that either. Top button missing.

GLAMOUR GIRL
Tatler-brand stilettos, non-weatherproof
coat, no trousers, French perfume,
discreetly made-up, impractical handbag…
works in an office; in the carriage, cheers
everyone else – male/grey/scruffy – up.

LEGAL PARODY
Boards, widely, at Shere, Oxshott, Pratt's
Bottom, pinstripes, puffy face, ruddy
cheeks, Bloody Train, airport aftershave,
musky sweat – City Gent v 2.0, knows it.

BLUESTOCKING
Head down, nose inside Diana Souhami's
biography of Radclyffe Hall, thighs all
her own, banana in her handbag.

MUSICAL YOUTH

Nods head, silently lipsynchs the beats
coming out of his MP3 player: this is
not a train, it's a club. Did that foot tap,
uncoolly, just for a moment?

SINGLEMAN

Not ready for work, in any way,
when he gets on at Stevenage… a
bit unshaven, a bit creased, a bit
underfed, a bit odorant; Stephen
King, a crumpled *Guardian*.

NEWLYWEDS

Self-satisifed couple, recently upscaled
from Streatham to suburbia, blithely
unaware of the future. Prone to
smiling, a snog, sharing a *Metro*.

NORBITON MAN

Angle-cornered executive briefcase
(contents: sandwiches, *A-Z*, spare batteries,
handkerchief), rainproof overcoat, polished
shoes, charcoal grey suit. Focused, ferocious
in his pussylike way, heroically pathetic.

TEXTIN INNIT

E likes 2 tap all d way 2 de fkin Loo innit.

MY COMMUTE: THE STOIC

Annabel Barber, Southgate to Green Park, July 1988–July 1990

I got my first job in London when I was 23. I had never lived there before. I hardly knew the place. I had naïve fantasies of finding a flat in one of those beautiful central London terraces, perhaps one of the ones with a garden in the middle of the square outside. I knew that Ramsay MacDonald had written with delight of the "calm dignity of pillared porticoes, bow-windows, broad steps and massive front doors." I imagined myself opening just such a door. But of course, I couldn't begin to afford anything dignified, pillared or massive. I had to move further out. And instead of groping my way timidly to the first affordable zone, I chose to move to the very fringe. I was working on Piccadilly, and so I elected to move somewhere that was on the Piccadilly Line, to give me a straight commute without the exhausting palaver of a change. I chose Southgate, almost at the end of the line, knowing that from there, I was certain to get a seat.

I did get one, every morning. And I would sit tight in it as, station by station, the carriage filled up and people began pressing in around my knees, their bags and briefcases knocking against my head, which was bowed, as I pretended to be oblivious to them, reading the *Meditations of Marcus Aurelius*, which is a book that epitomises for me those commuting days. I still have the copy. A small-format hardback with a tattered dust jacket. From it, I learned that "Nothing happens to anyone that he is not fitted by nature to bear," and that "It is not

death that a man should fear, but rather he should fear never beginning to live."

I liked the Piccadilly line. I liked its old-fashioned lifts and its station decorations, the tilework with the names picked out in brown. "Caledonian Road; Holloway Road; Arsenal; Finsbury Park…" I can still just about recite all the northbound stops. I even know that Arsenal was once called Gillespie Road. The old brown signs say so. Southgate station itself is elegant, Art Deco. A Charles Holden design of the 1930s, the era when travelling was glamorous instead of simply tiring and stressful.

Plenty of people were sceptical of my choice. "Southgate?" they would scoff. "Why live all the way out there? What's the point of coming to London if you're not going to be in the thick of things? You've got the worst of both worlds, neither urban nor rural." But for me, it worked. I looked forward to getting home in the evening, to the old village green which still preserved its stocks. I think that love of suburbia, for which the British are so tirelessly mocked, must lie deep within me too. There was a mansion at Southgate, built by Mr. Lipton, of tea fame. It was surrounded by a great park, for it had been Lipton's aim "never to have to behold another man's chimney pots" from his window. Southgate in my day was full of other men's chimney pots. From my own window, I saw little else. But I was happy there. I still feel a glow of residual warmth towards the Piccadilly Line. They were good days.

Timeline I

Artisans commute from Deir el-Medina to work on the tombs in the Valley of the Kings

16th century BC

5th century BC

Plato uses a water clock fitted with a special alarm to wake him up

Machu Picchu built by the Incas as a Garden City

12th century

1598

The word "coffee" enters the English language; its etymology could be from the Arabic *qahhwat al-bun* "wine of the bean" or an allusion to the Kingdom of Kaffa in Ethiopia, where coffee was first harvested

Traffic travelling north on London Bridge – the only bridge across the Thames - is ordered to stay on the left, establishing that law for England; the rule helped protect the bridge's monopoly

1722

1729

London's second bridge opens at Putney

Fortnum and Mason invents the first commuter food, the Scotch Egg, which becomes popular with rich coach travellers

1738

1803

The first horse-drawn public railway, the Surrey Iron Railway from Wandsworth to Croydon, is built

Regular steamboat services, mostly to downstream suburbs such as Greenwich, begin

1815

First horse-drawn omnibus runs between Paddington Green and the Bank of England in the City

1829

1820s

Short-stage coaches run to and from parishes on the edge of the built-up centre, including Camberwell, Clapham, Hackney, Islington and Paddington

14 Dec 1836

London Bridge Station opens on Tooley Street, generating walking commuter traffic on the bridge

8 February 1836

London's first passenger railway, the London and Greenwich, between Spa Road and Deptford, opens; Deptford is the first suburban railway station in the world; it is extended to London Bridge in the following months (and to Greenwich in April 1840)

2

AUBADE

We had a good slice of beef or two to our breakfast.

And from thence he took us into the wine-cellar;

where by my troth we were very merry,

and I drank too much wine, and all along had great and

particular kindness from Mr. Sayres, but I drank

so much wine that I was not fit for business.

The commute begins while the commuter is fast asleep. The hours in bed are timetabled like a night train. The dawn may be imagined as gradual as the slow rising of the sun, but in dreams, where time is compressed, the morning is always gathering pace.

When I lived on Norwood Road in Herne Hill, my small ground-floor flat backed on to the southern section of the Thameslink line between Blackfriars and south-west London. Mysterious trains made the house rumble in the small hours and before I willed myself to face the day, the early commuter services began to creep past in the half-light of waking.

I was brought up in Burtonwood, a small Lancashire village a mile to the south of the Liverpool-Manchester line, where Stephenson's *Rocket* was in service from 1830. Occasionally I fished for perch and roach at a pond nearby and I'd pause to watch the trains go by. On the way to town, a Deltic diesel train would sometimes pass beneath us as my dad's Mini sped over a high bridge that made my heart leap. Ever since then, trains have been a conduit to the exotic, though the exotic back then was only Earlestown and magnficient, faraway Manchester. But as an adult, the trains to and from Sutton and Luton were, from the lonely shore of the bed, faraway islands of possibility, worth my turning over for, and slipping back into sleep for a few more minutes.

The embankment rose steeply from behind the ivy-sundered fence that walled in our miniscule back yard. Breakfasting on cigarettes and coffee outside in the summer mornings, I'd look up to the slope, as densely wooded as a rainforest, a retreat for foxes, badgers, tits and blackbirds, snails, leeches, ladybirds, bees. When a train passed it was only visible as darker lines between the tree trunks, but there was the ancient mechanical sound, the scream of brakes or the clank-clank of something not properly oiled on a curve of iron poorly laid.

An aubade is a morning love song, the sleepier counterpart of the evening serenade. A poetic stock-in-trade, many bards have written them, from Shakespeare to Empson to Dickinson to Larkin. The latter would have appreciated that the word "aubade", typed into a search engine, comes up with lingerie before his own near-perfect poem.

Poets, like millionaires and dancers, may never have to see the dawn. As John Donne famously protested, when rudely awakened from his couch of love, "Busy old fool, unruly Sun, Why dost thou thus, through windows, and through curtains, call on us? Must to thy motions lovers' seasons run? Saucy pedantic wretch, go chide late schoolboys and sour prentices, Go tell courthuntsmen that the king will ride, call country ants to harvest offices." To slumber is to remain in the realm of the romantic, the poetic.

The murmur of talk radio, the teasmade, "dawn simulation light alarm clocks" and the natural properties of dawn – birdsong and breezes through an open window, sunshine muted by cotton drapes – can help ease our way into the glaring light of the day. How we try to play tricks on time and reality,

"In dreams, where time is compressed, the morning is always gathering pace"

resisting the call to shower, fuel up, set off. But the aubade, updated by Larkin, is unrelenting:

*Slowly light strengthens, and
    the room takes shape.
It stands plain as a wardrobe, what
    we know,
Have always known, know that
    we can't escape,
Yet can't accept. One side will
    have to go.
Meanwhile telephones crouch,
    getting ready to ring
In locked-up offices, and all
    the uncaring
Intricate rented world begins
    to rouse.
The sky is white as clay, with
    no sun.
Work has to be done.
Postmen like doctors go from
    house to house.*

From Aubade (1977) by Philip Larkin

The English morning, like its clay-coloured weather, has not changed much over the years, though now personal computers buzz, their screens blind and impassive, ready to ambush the worker. Offices are open ever earlier, baiting the redundancy-fearing enthusiast. And postmen come late, if at all.

A shower or a bath? Only the modern-day Donnes and Pepyses would dare indulge in a bubblesome soak, a commuting sin equivalent to breakfasting on Tokay and brioche. For most of us, the bathroom is a portal – a dreamer goes in, a worker emerges a few minutes later. And the twenty-first century commuter breakfast is rarely Mary Lamb's "social table". It's more probably food on the hop, panic-stricken cereals, burnt toast left to cool down by distractions, orange juice tainted by toothpaste, scalding tea; or a Berocca and, later on, a hung-over "Cornish" pasty at the terminus and a bucket of beige ersatz coffee.

The commuter can try to shower off sleep's aromas and generous, cold water splashes can hide the bed's creases. But it is a short distance from pillow to train and every morning thousands of dream-heavy passengers sit side by side or crush up against one other. Seats are in pairs, like beds, and thighs are against thighs and eye contact is sometimes made. Forced tenderness, obligatory contact, even shared sleeping... and then the non-accidental accidental touches and signs. The commuter at home is safe – from himself and from others – but once he leaves the den he is exposed ∎

Aubade

The lark now leaves his wat'ry nest,

And climbing shakes his dewy wings.

He takes this window for the East,

And to implore your light he sings—

Awake, awake! the morn will never rise

Till she can dress her beauty at your eyes.

The merchant bows unto the seaman's star,

The ploughman from the sun his season takes,

But still the lover wonders what they are

Who look for day before his mistress wakes.

Awake, awake! break thro' your veils of lawn!

Then draw your curtains, and begin the dawn!

William Davenant (1657)

Sleep: the problem

Contrary to the optimism of earlier sociological literature that predicted a "leisure revolution" driven by economic progress and technological automation in the workplace and household, societies where the majority of individuals experience a "glut of free time" have not yet eventuated. Phrases such as "time poverty" and "time famine", which are used to describe a shortage of time and an overwhelming acceleration of the rhythms of daily life, currently abound in popular discourse. Time and its allocations have become a matter of high politics in Britain and a lively debate over issues of work–life balance is currently unfolding in policy and academic circles…

The most common among competing explanations regarding "time poverty" has linked the phenomenon with the temporal operation of the labour market in post-industrial societies…. There is a negative correlation between sleep duration and the time workers spend commuting to and from the workplace which is near-linear. While only six per cent of men that did not report any commuting in their diaries are short sleepers, the increase is dramatic for men commuting more than two hours on the diary day, with 22 per cent obtaining insufficient sleep. The association between sleep duration and time spent commuting is also negative for female workers but not as pronounced as for men, with only 12 per cent of women that reported more than two hours of commuting obtaining short sleep duration.

… Short sleep durations are associated with age-related chronic disorders, diabetes, cardiovascular diseases and hypertension, weaker immune responses and self-rated poor health. A considerable number of epidemiological studies have found a strong relationship between shorter than average self-reported sleep durations (less than seven hours) and higher all-cause mortality and morbidity.

From "Lack of sleep, work and the long hours culture"
by Stella Chatzitheochari, Centre for Longitudinal Studies,
and Sara Arber, University of Surrey

Harry Palmer: commuter

I woke up saying to myself "today's the day" but I didn't feel much like getting out of bed just the same. I could hear the rain even before I drew the curtains back. December in London – the soot-covered tree outside was whipping itself into a frenzy.

I closed the curtains quickly, danced across the icy-cold lino, scooped up the morning's post and sat down heavily to wait while the kettle boiled. I struggled into the dark worsted and my only establishment tie – that's the red and blue silk with the square design – but had to wait forty minutes for a cab. They hate to come south of the Thames you see.

It always had made me feel a little self-conscious saying, "War Office" to cab drivers; at one time I had asked for a pub in Whitehall, or said "I'll tell you when to stop," just to avoid having to say it.

From The Ipcress File *(1962) by Len Deighton*

Car is king
Source: Department for Transport

HOW PEOPLE COMMUTE

	UK	London
By car	67%	36%
On foot	11%	9%
By bus/coach	9%	15%
By rail	5%	14%
Underground/light rail	n/a	19%
By bike	4%	4%

• Average journey time in the UK (2011): 28 minutes, an increase of 18% on 1995/97; the average journey to work for London residents takes just over 41 minutes, 48% longer than the national average.

• Men on average spend 19% longer commuting than women (29 minutes and 24 minutes respectively), reflecting differences in journey distance and mode.

• On average, commuting trips on foot take 18 minutes, by bicycle 22 minutes, by car 24 minutes, by bus 41 minutes, and by surface rail 69 minutes.

• Commuters in the UK travel, on average, 1,266 miles/year.

Alain de Botton and the swan of sleep

It is six o'clock on a late-July morning, in a village fifty kilometres from the office, in the Berkshire countryside. To define what is painfully coming to an end, thanks to the pitiless insistence of an electronic chirrup, as "being asleep" doesn't scratch the surface of what has really been going on for the last seven hours, ever since one of the accountants I am shadowing lost contact with her conscious self while watching a regional news item and was transported off on the back of the swan of sleep.

She may only have been lying under a duvet, in a room undisturbed except by the occasional sweep of car headlamps across the ceiling, and yet she was all the while being shuttled on turbulent journeys animated by unexpected faces and emotions.

…Once the alarm has rung, the accountant has little choice but to head for the bathroom without doing justice to her visions. Sentimental associations and impossible longings are shut down, and the self is reassembled as an apparently coherent entity, with stable commitments and a prescribed future.
From The Pleasures and Sorrows of Work, *VIII: Accountancy (2010)*

How many Londoners listen to…
The capital's most popular radio stations
Source: Rajar – 2012/Q2

BBC Radio 4:	2,726,000
BBC Radio 2:	2,202,000
Capital FM:	2,072,000
Magic 105.4:	1,951,000
Heart:	1,798,000
BBC Radio 1:	1,750,000
KISS:	1,740,000
Classic FM:	1,269,000
BBC Radio 5 live:	1,247,000
Absolute Radio:	974,000
LBC 97.3:	809,000
talkSPORT:	661,000

Sex-urbia

For a man facing both Monday morning and utter defeat he did not feel too bad. The morning sun, beaming like a cheap salesman, burst from the direction of Breakspear Crematorium (a reminder that Nicholas Breakspear, the only English pope, was of these parts), there was a wide optimism about the sky and the grinning fields, and the girl from Cowacre, the one with the bum like a deftly closed tulip, was walking by on her way to the station.

Andrew's double-glazed kitchen window was higher than all the others at Plummers Park, for his four-bedroomed house, garage and carport, Blo-hole heating, bland picture windows, sun patio, old tree incorporated into the garden wall, was on the prow of Upmeadow. From the sitting room a variety of sunsets could be witnessed through the seasons, a ritual dipping which, the estate agent had assured him, would be an asset if he ever decided to sell. From the place where he stood he could look, in fact he had no choice but to look, out on to the flat roofs of all the other houses on the estate, scattered in the valley like bamboo rafts on some wide eastern river.

The girl from Cowacre wore a pale shirt, tight across her brassy little breasts, their noses prodding through the material. His coffee-cup immobilised at the tilt, he watched her stride by, her legs long, her face clean and confident as the sun, and waited in anticipation for the promised view of her backside.

From Tropic of Ruislip *(1974) by Leslie Thomas*

SLEEP WELL?

WELL NOW YOU CAN WAKE UP WELL TOO

USE THE TIMER OPTION AND TURN HUE INTO YOUR MORNING WAKE UP CALL. IT CERTAINLY BEATS THE SHOCK OF AN ALARM CLOCK

Set your lights to gradually brighten over time, waking you up in a rather more civilised fashion. Better still, why not create a scene from the image of a dawn sun and turn Hue into your own personal sunrise? That's something worth getting up for.

Advert for Philips 'Hue' lighting, 2013

Pepys at breakfast

FRIDAY 6 JANUARY 1659/60
This morning Mr. Sheply and I did eat
our breakfast at Mrs. Harper's (my
brother John being with me) upon a
cold turkey-pie and a goose. From
thence I went to my office, where we
paid money to the soldiers till one
o'clock, at which time we made an end,
and I went home and took my wife
and went to my cosen, Thomas Pepys,
and found them just sat down to
dinner, which was very good; only
the venison pasty was palpable beef,
which was not handsome.

MONDAY 7 MAY 1660
This morning Captain Cuttance sent
me 12 bottles of Margate ale. Three
of them I drank presently with some
friends in the Coach. My Lord went
this morning about the flag-ships in a
boat, to see what alterations there must
be, as to the arms and flags. He did

give me order also to write for silk flags
and scarlett waistcloathes. For a rich
barge; for a noise of trumpets, 1 and a
set of fidlers.

**WEDNESDAY 15 JANUARY
1661/62**
This morning Mr. Berkenshaw came
again, and after he had examined
me and taught me something in my
work, he and I went to breakfast in my
chamber upon a collar of brawn, and
after we had eaten, asked me whether
we had not committed a fault in eating
to-day; telling me that it is a fast day
ordered by the Parliament.

WEDNESDAY 24 APRIL 1661
Waked in the morning with my head
in a sad taking through the last night's
drink, which I am very sorry for; so rose
and went out with Mr. Creed to drink
our morning draft, which he did give
me in chocolate to settle my stomach.

MONDAY 9 SEPTEMBER 1661
To the Privy Seal in the morning, but
my Lord did not come, so I went with
Capt. Morrice at his desire into the
King's Privy Kitchin to Mr. Sayres
the Master-Cooke, and there we had
a good slice of beef or two to our
breakfast. And from thence he took us
into the wine-cellar; where by my troth
we were very merry, and I drank too
much wine, and all along had great and
particular kindness from Mr. Sayres,
but I drank so much wine that I was
not fit for business.
From Samuel Pepys' Diary (1659–61)

Ten Commandments of Commuting

I
Thou shalt avoid prolonged eye contact.

II
Thou shalt not kiss or caress anyone.

III
Thou shalt not be cheery and sociable.

IV
Thou oughtest not to complain or express
surprise at delays.

V
Thou wilt frown at holidaymakers and their baggage and
untimely boarding of the morning train.

VI
Thou shalt look down at thy freesheet when a pregnant
woman boards.

VII
Thou shalt place a banana skin or empty coffee cup on
the seat beside thine.

VIII
Thou shalt deny having farted by looking about the carriage silently.

IX
Thou shalt balance on one leg, or one heel, or ball, or use an elbow
to support thy torso, or move contorted and uncomplaining,
so long as thou disturbest not thy fellow sufferers.

X
Thou wilt not feel like a Thou so much as an It or a Thing –
the children of suburbia, cast out on the eternal
two-way Exodus.

THE CITY GENT: STRIPPED

2. THE TIE

"Daily the modern man endures this civilised abuse, to place a blade against his throat and his head inside a noose." Anon.

Penis pointer or flaccid fashion statement? The tie, if humble in appearance, tends to provoke extreme opinions. Adding a flash of colour to the drabbest office uniform, it's also the clerical noose, the effete gesture of rebellion, the straightener of the soul.

The history of the necktie is long and knotty. Ancient examples include the silk cloths tied round the necks of the terracotta soldiers buried with Chinese emperor Shih Huang Ti in 210 BC. On Trajan's Column in Rome, erected in AD 113, legionaries are depicted with neckcloths, possibly to soak up sweat, or possibly to deflect sword blows. Some scholars believe Roman orators wore mufflers to keep their larynxes warm.

In 1635, Croatian mercenaries fighting for King Louis XIII in Paris sported coloured scarves around their necks. Admiring Parisians began to imitate them, adopting neck scarves *"à la croate"* – which led to the birth of the cravat, which in turn evolved into the necktie.

In the eighteenth century, neckerchiefs had a twofold function: to keep the wearer warm and his collar clean; Regency

fashionista Beau Brummel is known to have worn ruffled ascots, which quickly became the standard in England. At the end of the nineteenth century, rowers at the Universtity of Oxford wore decorative hatbands; one legend asserts that a rower removed his and tied it around his neck. True or false, since that time ties have been associated with membership of a club, military regiments and schools and clubby stripes have survived the evolution of the tie from the Bold look of the 1940s to the 1960s' kipper to the narrow, conservative style currently in vogue.

Bond Street, Jermyn Street and Savile Row, formerly areas where military officers and politicians had their residences, evolved as shirt-making and general tailoring centres at the end of the eighteenth century. Those seeking to ape the apparel of the City Gent can pick up silk ties at traditional outlets like Turnbull & Asser, Benson & Clegg, Drakes and Emmett.

In a book from 1818, *"Neckclothitania; or, Tietania, an essay on starchers"* – the nickname for cravats – written by *"one of the cloth"*, we have a summary of the qualities a tie can add to a man's appearance:

What an apparent superiority does not a starcher give to a man? It gives him a look of hauteur and greatness, which can scarcely be acquired otherwise – This is

produced solely by the austere rigidity of the cravat, which so far, by any means, from yielding to the natural motions of the head, forms a strong support to the cheeks. It pushes them up, and gives a rotundity of appearance to the whole figure [face], thereby unquestionably giving a man the air of being puffed up with pride, vanity, and conceit, (very necessary, nay, indispensable qualifications for a man of fashion) and appearing as quite towering over the rest of mankind, and holding his fellow-creatures covered with the deep disgrace of his disgust.

I need only appeal to any common observer, to prove the veracity of the above assertions – Let any person take a stroll up and down some fashionable street of the metropolis, at the proper time of day, and remark the men who do and who do not wear starchers: What a conscious sense of their own superiority in the former! What a full conviction of their own paltriness and insignificance in the latter!!

MY COMMUTE: THE TRAIN DRIVER

Andrew Cook, Southern Railway, 2012–present

I've been a driver for ten years, so am still a new boy compared to some on the railway. I live near Sevenoaks and work out of Selhurst Depot, south-east London. I drive in and out of London Bridge and Victoria taking commuters to work in the morning and the sometimes well-oiled folks on their return journey home. I often start very early (silly o'clock I call it) getting up at 2am to be at work for 3:46am for some of the earliest starts. This means that I bring the first train out of the depot all clean and ready for our passengers' journey. It might mean driving out to places like Purley, Epsom or Croydon to take the first train of the day up to London. I'm happy so long as my cab heating works.

I'm alone up front, but there's no time to be lonely – too much to concentrate on. I'm quite a cheerful person, and if I ever look unhappy it's because I'm focused on doing the job safely. As I pull up alongside the platform early in the morning there are many sights that greet me. That early, not everyone is fully awake. I see yawning people with that "just got out of bed" look. But I have to ask myself: are they standing too close to the edge of the platform? Is that person wearing earphones and not aware that my train is approaching?

I see girls with "just washed" long hair doing their make-up, looking glum at the prospect of another day in the city. Many are reading the *Metro* newspaper. All are standing in little groups along the platform next to where the doors will be when the train stops. I have to be careful to make sure I stop my train in the right place. If I don't stop in the usual place, everyone has to shuffle around, elbows at the ready with that steely determination to get "their seat" on the carriage that gives them the best shot of getting off the train nearest to the station exit. I check to make sure I open the doors on the correct side of the train. If I get that wrong the consequences could be serious.

Most trains now have automated audio and visual announcements but sometimes these systems break down. If that happens I make announcements manually. I would love to be able to engage with passengers by making funny and helpful comments – but as I'm no good at that I just play it straight. There are some drivers that do make very funny comments while still covering the important information.

The usual "rush hour" times of 07:00–10:00 and 16:00–19:00 are the busiest, when all trains are full and a lot are pretty much at bursting point. Stations like East Croydon, Clapham Junction and of course Victoria and London Bridge are extremely busy for most of the day as they are major transport interchanges.

We aim to run on time. One of the things that irks me (and I think many drivers) is the fact that some passengers will tap their watches at you when you roll down the platform when you're late ("Got a new watch?"

I say to myself), but then all crowd around one set of doors to queue up to get on the train. It would be much better if they spread themselves out along the platform to "use all available doors", then it would make loading that much quicker and less frustrating for all concerned. It's even worse on the way home in the evening rush hour.

Driving a train doesn't mean that you have to be looking at the track all the time without taking your eyes off it but when there's a little time between stations, for example on the way to Guildford, I do like to look at the countryside and what it has to offer. Llamas in the field, ducks crossing the foot-crossing with their ducklings (glad I missed running them over), kestrels hovering, buzzards soaring, pheasants and other game birds and horses too.

Driving trains at the weekend is a very different experience. You generally see happy people going out for the day, kids waving at the train drivers and getting excited when I wave back.

My advice to commuters: get on and off the train using ALL available doors promptly. Arrive at the platform late and you'll get left behind. Stand well back from the edge of the platform – you might not think you're putting yourself in danger, but one slip, trip or fall when I'm bringing my train in could mean more than just a grazed knee – seeing people too close to the edge scares the life out of me!

Timeline II

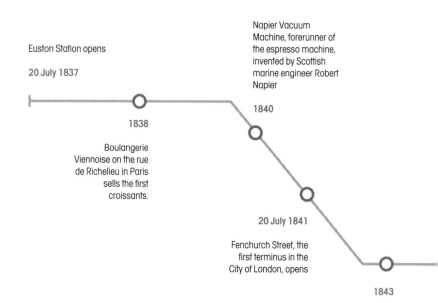

Euston Station opens

20 July 1837

Napier Vacuum
Machine, forerunner of
the espresso machine,
invented by Scottish
marine engineer Robert
Napier

1840

1838

Boulangerie
Viennoise on the rue
de Richelieu in Paris
sells the first
croissants.

20 July 1841

Fenchurch Street, the
first terminus in the
City of London, opens

1843

The Thames Tunnel
designed by Sir Marc
Brunel opens as a
pedestrian tunnel and
is later used for
underground trains.

Charles Pearson, a
London Solicitor,
begins to promote the
development of an
underground railway

1845

Thomas Tilling goes
into business running
horse-drawn buses
out of Walworth; he
will later introduce
fixed stops and
timetables

1846

Waterloo Station opens

11 July 1848

14 October 1845

King's Cross
Station opens

1847

French inventor Antoine
Redier patents the
adjustable mechanical
alarm clock

3

SUBURB

I know a land where the wild flowers grow

Near, near at hand if by train you go,

Metro-land, Metro-land.

Meadows sweet have a golden glow...

weet suburbia. Jerry Leadbetter in *The Good Life*, Reggie Perrin at Norbiton station. Iain Sinclair's orbiting around the M25 and Patrick Keiller's disembodied flaneuring with a film camera. Betjeman and Bucks. Hancock and "East Cheam". The Kinks, Bowie and The Cure. The suburbs have their psalmists and the home counties their minstrels.

It was not always like this. Peter Ackroyd, in his expansive *London: The Biography*, after observing that, from the seventeenth century, the city expanded "organically", unevenly and inexorably, notes that "this natural glut of buildings and people provoked sensations of disgust and dismay. It seemed to threaten the identity of the city itself." Trollope certainly thought so. By 1857, in *The Three Clerks*, he was writing about how difficult it was "to say where the suburbs of London come to an end, and where the country begins. The railways, instead of enabling Londoners to live in the country, have turned the country into a city. London will soon assume the shape of a great starfish. The old town, extending from Poplar to Hammersmith, will be the nucleus, and the various railway lines will be the projecting rays."

If only he'd known what was to come. Because Paul Barker, in his quietly iconoclastic *The Freedoms of Suburbia* states a simple truth when he says that Oxford is to London today what Hampstead was to the city of a century ago. Townies and gownies travel down the motorway in a coach called the Oxford Tube, but the journeys they are making are no different from those made by 1950s' Hampstead literati, who travelled to and fro on the Northern Line. "With its suburbs and exurbs, from Oxford to Southend, from Cambridge to Brighton, London is now a 100-mile city."

In origin, the "suburbs" are the areas immediately outside the confines of the nuclear city, the parts that lay just beyond the walls. As Peter Ackroyd puts it, "they were once the spillings and scourings of the city, unhappy and insalubrious. The 'subarbes' contained precisely that which had been banished

*"The suburbs turned
Felicity Kendal into a sex-
symbol and David Bowie
into a star-gazer"*

from the town, the 'stink' industries, brothels, leper hospitals, theatres, so that the area beyond the walls was in some way deemed threatening or lawless."

Not threatening or lawless any longer, perhaps, but definitely "beyond the pale": the London mind still maintains erect an intact ghost London Wall, placed either neatly around the Circle line or envisioned as a sort of bendy rectangle with its long sides along the Thames and Euston Road and shorter edges at the A220 and A10, or if the mind is feeling bounteous – and happens to live in Brixton, Dalston or Fulham – around the line that demarcates Zones 2 and 3 of the transport network.

Though more than a century ago, HG Wells and Yeats lived in, respectively, Bromley and Bedford Park – the latter regarded at the time as an archetypal suburb. Writers and artists have generally liked to stress their association with the centre, the fun part of town. Modernists only went beyond the Circle

Line when the "real" country summoned, and most post-war writers have drawn the line of their London somewhere near Swiss Cottage. The best known bard of the outer boroughs, JG Ballard, has exploited the dystopian potential of the suburban fantasy. His last novel, 2006's *Kingdom Come*, opens with the provocative line: "The suburbs dream of violence."

In deference to the intellectual elite, the liberal Londoner still likes to signal his disdain for the in-betweenness of the towns and villages beyond the M25, the train-user, the imagined *Standard*-reader. The (leafy) suburbs challenge the (built) urbanite's self-image. They stir extreme opinions. Those who live in Zones 3 and 4 are particularly anxious to stress their disdain for the suburbs. How many times have you heard the commonplace: "I love the city and the country, just not the bit in between"? In the 2002 film *The Hours*, screenwriter David Hare plays to this prejudice. Virginia Woolf tells Leonard that she cannot bear the "suffocating anaesthetic of the suburbs", preferring, indeed needing, "the violent jolt of the Capital." When she adds, "if it is a choice between Richmond and death, I choose death," it's a joke, on her, not a psychogeographical maxim.

Suburbanites, for their part, have been guilty of capital-fear. With each generation, a new gang of vehement Nimbys protests the London-isation of their lifestyles. Right now, the danger zone is a loop through Walton-on-Thames, Swanley, Brentwood, Borehamwood and Slough. Here some residents want to stay safe in their Ashvales and High Streets, seemingly blind to the most common street name in the sticks: London Road.

For all these historical prejudices and mental walls, the seduction is two-way. The home counties beckon walkers on Saturday mornings and many city-dwellers ultimately decide to give up the Costcutters and bus stops and embrace the green belt. The suburbs turned Felicity Kendal into a sex-symbol and David Bowie into a star-gazer. Keillor, in *London* (1994), claims that "London is a city under siege from a suburban government," yet his film tacitly acknowledges that any poetry to be found in the capital will be found far away from the bobbies and busbies of the tourist-jammed centre. We all thrive on ambivalence.

Which is just as well, as most people in London, and in Britain, live in suburbs – residential sprawls and nexuses connected by mass transit systems to workplaces and leisure spaces. It's more a question of what kind of suburb you live in – one with a few parks and canals and a short Tube journey, or one with chalky hills, sheep and an extortionately expensive rail pass. Paul Barker champions the residential choice of suburbanites – who, he says, amount to 84 per cent of Britons. "Suburbia is derided by everyone – except the millions who live there, and shop happily at the nearest mall. It must be doing something right… Suburbia is a great triumph of non-planning. There has been no great, overarching, even dictatorial vision. Much has happened by accident. A city is not a computer program. It is very hard to tweak it the way you wish. It has a life of its own, to try to talk about cities, without talking frankly about their suburbs and their appeal, is completely bizarre."

The popular notion of London's villages derives from the fact that 200 years ago there were fields and rivers flowing between each of the inner and outer boroughs. Suburbanisation has not killed this, but has spread the anarchy ever further. Perhaps London's best book – its autobiography – is the *A-Z*. It records the tangled streets, broken horizons, the curves and dead ends. This labyrinth seems at odds with the linearity of the thin black arcs of the railway lines that try to connect it all up. The suburbs begin at the river, just beyond the railway termini.

You buy an *A-Z* when you get your home. You find your street and your new workplace on the map. You put the book away and you get on with the commuting. One day you will explore everything ■

The Home Counties

London was the world's biggest city during the nineteenth century. The eight 'ancient counties' closest to the metropolis – usually called 'home counties', a term derived from local courts – evolved and became richer than the rest of England by providing London with food and other goods and services. From 1889 they encircled the County of London, but in 1965, with the establishment of Greater London, parts of Essex, Hertfordshire, Kent and Surrey were absorbed, while Middlesex disappeared. Always more populated than other pastoral regions, the counties of south-eastern England have grown significantly in recent times, and continue to attract economic migrants. The commuter network, more than any other factor, has deepened their relationship with London and as the twenty-first century capital looks skyward in its architecture, we can expect the horizontal city to stretch to the limits allowed by transport and time.

Woe unto them that join house to house, that lay field to field, till there is no place.

Isaiah 5:8

Populations of the home counties and London
Sources: the 1801, 1901 and 2001 census results

	1801	1901	2001
Buckinghamshire	107,444	195,905	479,024
Hertfordshire	97,577	250,162	1,033,977
Essex	227,682	1,085,771	1,310,835
Berkshire	109,215	252,571	800,118
Middlesex	818,129	3,585,323	n/a
Surrey	79,377	675,774	1,059,000
Kent	308,667	1,348,841	1,579,200
Sussex	159,311	605,202	1,245,936
London	959,310	4,536,267	7,172,036

Sweet suburbia: a potted (aspidistra) history

How disease, avarice and homesickness led to punk songs and super prime properties.

Until medieval times, the only place to be if you belonged to the elite was within London's walls. But from the thirteenth century onwards, recurring outbreaks of bubonic plague prompted a series of migrations away from the capital. Edward Platt, in his *Leadville: A Biography of the A40*, claims the suburb was born as "a rural isolation ward".

The suburban mindset was established in the eighteenth century when affluent private individuals – many of them Londoners – enclosed more and more of the common land. This gave rise to the notions of "town" and "country" and what Raymond Williams calls the "suburban or dormitory dream". This enduring pastoral fantasy idealised rural life and turned it into a commodity.

In the Victorian era, cholera and typhus struck London. The middle classes began to look for homes in the suburbs. With the building of the railways, office workers, brokers, bankers and lawyers followed in the wake of the country seat-owning aristocrats. The working classes migrated too, filling in the gaps between the city and what used to be the countryside. The population of outer London grew from 414,000 in 1861 to 2,045,000 in 1901.

By the middle of the twentieth century, one-time villages like Hampstead, Chiswick and Camberwell had become a continuous sprawl that extended deep into the home counties. Company headquarters, film studios and universities were uprooted from the centre to become established in the periphery.

In the 1970s, the suburban lifestyle began to fascinate television writers and punk musicians. The former – middle class and metropolitan – poked fun and kept the fantasy alive. The punks, who actually came from the dormitories, screamed out at the boredom and the banality.

Nowadays many dormitory towns have as many incoming commuters as outgoing ones. Like a series of little Londons, they hum with the sound of cars, railways and jet engines. They pride themselves on their chain stores, impossible parking regimes, sophisticated gastronomy and convenient proximity to the motorway network. Garden centres, the remnants of ancient woodland, disputed footpaths, and country parks and inns both ersatz and enduring encourage the conservation of the pastoral illusion.

To the pastoral, punk and sitcom tropes the 2000s added a new one: "super prime" property values. Everyone seems to love or loathe the idea of the suburb these days. Everyone seems to love or loathe the idea of the city too. It's as if the old London wall had gone up again but this time round, the plague is on both sides.

Tend your garden

And you will there have a little garden, with a shallow well from which you can easily draw water, without need of a rope, to bedew your weakly plants. There make your abode, a friend of the mattock, tending a trim garden fit to feast a hundred Pythagoreans.

From Satire 3: 226–9 (late first century AD) by Juvenal, trans. GG Ramsay

A grassy knoll

"Where is the green-house to be?"
"Upon the knoll behind the house. The old walnut trees are all come down to make room for it. It will be a very fine object from many parts of the park, and the flower-garden will slope down just before it, and be exceedingly pretty."

From Sense and Sensibility (1811) by Jane Austen

Seventies' Suburbia: a culture crammer

The Good Life (1975–8)
The Fall and Rise of Reginald Perrin (1976–9)
Abigail's Party (1977)

Leslie Thomas *Tropic of Ruislip* (1974)
Julian Barnes *Metroland* (1980)
Hanif Kureishi *The Buddha of Suburbia* (1990): set in the 1970s

O Level *East Sheen* (1978)
The Skids *Sweet Suburbia* (1978
The Members *The Sound of the Suburbs* (1979)
The Leyton Buzzards *Saturday Night*
(Beneath the Plastic Palm Trees) (1979)

Desirable Dormitories

Don't believe estate agents: these Word Clouds will help you to find your dream home. Can you match each Cloud to its suburb: Bishop's Stortford; Cheshunt; Chigwell; Great Missenden; Surbiton; Purley; Tunbridge Wells? (Answers below)

1.

Butterflies **Hammer** **HS2**
Chilterns ROBERT LOUIS STEPHENSON
10,138 Roald Dahl 46 mins to Marylebone

2. 38,158 THAMES
Enid Blyton **Thomas Hardy**
William Holman Hunt
TOM 18 mins to Waterloo BARBARA
John Everett Millais **charity shops**
SEETHING WELLS

3.

Ermine Street

MERIDIAN TESCO 51,998

Lotus

POSH SPICE

23 mins to Liverpool Street

Cliff Richard
TEMPLE BAR
Laura Trott
Wolsey
Spurs

4. Rita Tushingham
market town STANSTED
gorgeous the dog 38,078
38 mins to Liverpool Street Cecil Rhodes
Flux of Pink Indians MONARCHISM

5.

Bobby Moore

Ashley Cole BIRDS OF A FEATHER
SPURS 34 minutes to Bank
12,699 Change at Woodford
LEYTON ORIENT Epping Forest
Dogging **ALAN SUGAR**
Barnaby Rudge

Dick Turpin
Ye Olde King's Head

7. **UTOPIA**
23 mins to London Bridge
Terry and June CR8
NUDGE NUDGE
Peter Cushing
NIGEL HARMAN Bucks Fizz
footballers' wives
Derren Brown
Mr ANGRY 72,000
Brotherhood of Man

Webb Estate

6.

Earnest

William Makepeace Thackeray
PEOPLE'S LIBERATION FRONT
Daily Telegraph 115,2oo

46 minutes to London Bridge

ROYAL
Cibber
GARDENING
DISGUSTED

I know a land

I know a land where the wild flowers grow
Near, near at hand if by train you go,
Metro-land, Metro-land.
Meadows sweet have a golden glow
Hills are green as the vales below
In Metro-land, Metro-land.

Leafy dell and woodland fair,
Land of love and hope and peace,
Land where all your troubles cease,
Metro-land, Metro-land,
Waft, O waft me there.

George Robert Sims (1847–1922)

Rus in suburbe

NATIVE TOPOGRAPHY AND RURAL HISTORY

Nine Mile Ride, Wokingham. As straight as a Roman Road, this now heavily trafficked, tree-lined thoroughfare was built by King George III on a long wide cut through Windsor Forest previously used by Queen Anne who – unable or unwilling to ride due to being overweight – would follow the hunt in her carriage.

Penn Street Village in the Chilterns in Buckinghamshire has a Brythonic name, "penn" meaning hill in the Celtic language of the Britons. When deprived of ancient woodland, modern suburbs often concoct fake pastoral, as in Shadbolt Close in Worcester Park, which takes its name from a "lost" Bedfordshire village. See also: Saddlers Court, Epsom; Chalk Lane, East Horsley; Rector Lane, Shere; Ash Grove, Guildford; Manor Road, Walton-on-Thames; Verulam Road, St Albans; The Briars, High Wycombe.

SUBURBAN PLANTING

Acacia Avenue, Leytonstone. Yes, there is a real one here, and another in Hillingdon, and another just off the A10 in Tottenham, and at least six more in Greater London. In the 1945 film *29 Acacia Avenue*, the cliché of a middle-class suburban street was established; since then, it has appeared as the location of a brothel – at No. 22 – in the Iron Maiden song "22 Acacia Avenue" and the home, as 29 Acacia Road, Nuttytown, of Eric Wimp aka

Bananaman in comic strips in *Nutty*, *The Beano* and *The Dandy*. The acacia tree grows wild along the Nile and in the Australian Outback. See also: Cedars Avenue, Rickmansworth; Maple Road, Redhill; Stipularis Drive, Hayes; Robinia Avenue, Gravesend.

LANDOWNERS, LORDS AND OTHER NOTABLES

Chertsey Street, Guildford. Chertsey Abbey was a Benedictine Abbey founded in the sixth century at Chertsey in Surrey. There are Chertsey roads and streets and the occasional avenue across west and south-west London and around the Surrey Hills. Devereux Way, Billericay alludes to the family name of the dukes of Essex. Claremont Street, Esher and many other local Claremonts around Staines, Surbiton and West Byfleet reference the estate of Claremont, a fine Palladian mansion built in 1708 by Sir John Vanbrugh, just south of Esher. Orpington has an Augustine Road and a Darwin Close, celebrating the first archbishop of Canterbury and the local resident who upended the Church in the nineteenth century.

WELCOME TO UTOPIA

Midsummer Boulevard, Milton Keynes. In the most parodied of all exurbs, Milton Keynes, you can stand on the corner of Midsummer Boulevard and Upper Fourth Street. The coordinates meld some specious New York fantasy, a hint of Paris and a touch of old-world leafiness. See also: Fourth Avenue,

Harlow; Kyoto Terrace, Havant, Hampshire; Safety Drive, Poole (formerly Salamander Road); Avenue One, Letchworth Garden City; The Quadrangle, Welwyn Garden City; Arterial Road, West Thurrock.

MIGRATION AND MODERNITY
Fleming Way in Tonbridge, and also in other Kent towns, harks back to Flemish artisans who arrived as refugees in the sixteenth century. Jewry Street in central Winchester has its roots in migrants during the medieval era. In modern times, Khadija Walk, Lewisham, is named after Mohammed's first wife. Ashanti Mews in Hackney honours a major ethnic group and an area of Ghana. Polonez Court, Swindon, shares its name with a Communist-era car maker. See also: Yoga Way, Sutton, south London.

Home by the railway

My dear wife Carrie and I have just been a week in our new house, "The Laurels," Brickfield Terrace, Holloway – a nice six-roomed residence, not counting basement, with a front breakfast-parlour. We have a little front garden; and there is a flight of ten steps up to the front door, which, by-the-by, we keep locked with the chain up. Cummings, Gowing, and our other intimate friends always come to the little side entrance, which saves the servant the trouble of going up to the front door, thereby taking her from her work. We have a nice little back garden which runs down to the railway. We were rather afraid of the noise of the trains at first, but the landlord said we should not notice them after a bit, and took £2 off the rent. He was certainly right; and beyond the cracking of the garden wall at the bottom, we have suffered no inconvenience.

From The Diary of a Nobody *(1892) by George Grossmith and Weedon Grossmith*

Train tweet
janine jorgensen @j_ninej

Nose picker (and eater), crisp packet licker, dragon boat racer, banana dumper, priest #londoncommute

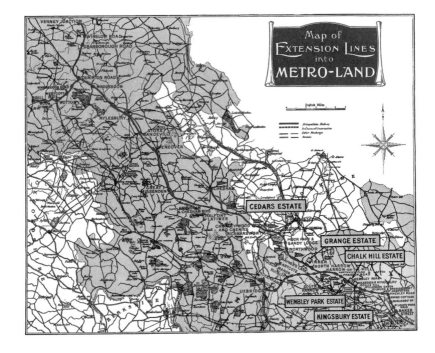

Metro-land brochure, 1927

This is a good parcel of English soil in which to
build home and strike root, inhabited from old, as
witness the line of camps on the hill tops and
confused mounds amongst the woods, the great
dykes which crossed it east and west, the British
trackways, the Roman road aslant the eastern
border, the packhorse ways worn deep into the
hillsides, the innumerable fieldpaths which mark
the labourers' daily route from hamlet to farm. The
new settlement of Metro-land proceeds apace, the
new settlers thrive amain.

Julian Barnes on Metroland

"Où habites-tu?" they would ask year after year, drilling us for French orals; and I always would smirkingly reply, *"J'habite Metroland."*

It sounded better than Eastwick, stranger than Middlesex; more like a concept than a place where you shopped. And so, of course, it was. As the Metropolitan Railway had pushed westwards in the 1880s, a thin corridor of land was opened up with no geographical or ideological unity: you lived there because it was an area easy to get out of. The name Metroland – adopted during the First World War both by estate agents and by the railway itself – gave the string of rural suburbs a spurious integrity.

In the early 1960s, the Metropolitan Line (by which the purist naturally meant the Watford, Chesham and Amersham branches) still retained some of its original separateness. The rolling-stock, painted a distinctive mid-brown, had remained unchanged for sixty years; some of the bogeys, my Ian Allen spotter's book informed me, had been running since the early 1890s. The carriages were high and square, with wooden running boards; the compartments were luxuriously wide by modern standards, and the breadth of the seats made one marvel at Edwardian femoral development. The backs of the seats were raked at an angle which implied that in the old days the trains had stopped for longer at the stations.

Above the seats were sepia photographs of the line's beauty spots – Sandy Lodge Golf Course, Pinner Hill, Moor Park, Chorleywood. Most of the original fittings remained: wide, loosely strung luggage racks with coat-hooks curving down from their support struts; broad leather window straps, and broad leather straps to stop the doors from swinging all the way back to the hinges; a chunky, gilded figure on the door, 1 or 3; a brass fingerplate backing the brass door handle; and, engraved on the plate, in a tone of command or seductive invitation, the slogan "Live in Metroland".

From Metroland *(1980)*

Samuel Beckett on Habit

Habit is a compromise effected between the individual and his environment, or between the individual and his own organic eccentricities, the guarantee of a dull inviolability, the lightning-conductor of his existence. Habit is the ballast that chains the dog to his vomit. Breathing is habit. Life is habit.
From *Proust* (1930)

A Hornchurch Commuter

It's Winter and I leave my home in darkness
to schlep down Suttons Gardens, Stations Lane,
then past the rows of houses lost to commerce:
the florist, cabbies, bookies, café, train.

They call this game the rat race but it's not —
these sad and silty mornings pocked with sighs;
there's nothing fast about this way of life —
just deep ruts cut slow into the mind's eye.

I spend my Mondays living for the weekend —
who doesn't here, eh, that's the way it works;
that's why we brought our families to the suburbs
to live on London's green and pleasant skirt.

Inside this fizzing fence of motorway,
our tiny crumbs of Essex neatly mortgaged,
a low-rent Metroland for boys done good;
a place to deckchair doze in heavy August.

And for that right we clatter down these traintracks
through greyish sprawl from Dagenham to Bow
where London's mouth lies waiting. Grin and bear it:
inhale, exhale then underground you go.

From Mondeo Man *(2013) by Luke Wright*

The Betjeman line

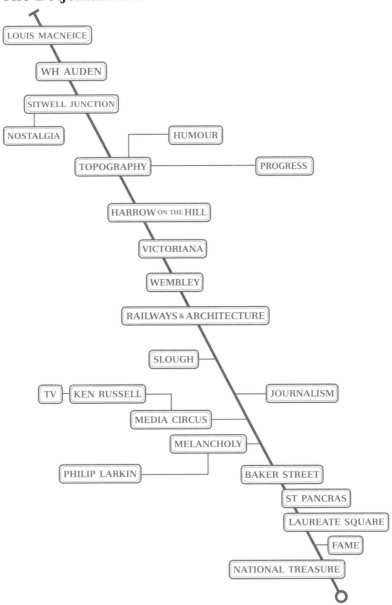

Betjeman: the bard of the burbs

John Betjeman (1906–84) is almost as famous for his poems about London's northwestern suburbs (sold to homebuyers in the 1920s as Metro-land) as he is for summoning bombs to be dropped on Slough. If his work is sometimes batted around as a literary justification for nostalgic excess, Nimbyish ruraphilia and a sort of middle-class, middle-aged middlingness, it hides deeper thoughts and social currents.

Sensitive, socially embarrassed by his parents' household goods business and educated – and bullied – at Highgate public school (where TS Eliot gave classes), Betjeman flopped out of Oxford and went on to work, briefly, at the *Evening Standard*. He wrote travel guides for motorists before committing himself to poetry. His verse, and his readings of it in broadcasts, was accessible, often humorous and imbued with an acute sense of time and place. Conservative and fogeyish, he fashioned a sort of whimsical melancholia to lament the passing of an England that he'd never actually lived in.

London's commuter railways and suburbs – symbolising technology and a botched rural idyll – were perfect material. "Early Electric! With what radiant hope/Men formed this many-branched electrolier," he gasps in "Baker Street Station Buffet", surveying Metroland's broken dreams. In "Harrow on the Hill" the humdrum becomes mock-heroic: "And the rumble of the railway/Is the thunder of the rollers." In "Middlesex" dainty Elaine hurries

"down the concrete station" into a county where "a few surviving hedges/ Keep alive our lost Elysium". For him, suburbia reflects life's deeper losses.

A critically acclaimed television programme, *Metro-land* (1973), produced by Edward Mirzoeff, connected Betjeman with that corner of the world for a mass audience. A founding member of the Victorian Society and a poet laureate, he was the last living British poet who could genuinely be called a household name.

A stalwart of the Establishment, the *Daily Telegraph* and Radio 4, his poetry appeals to the kinds of reader who disdain John Clare and only like the funny bits in Larkin and Eliot. But Betjeman's poems pepper this compendium – and provide its title – because they record the essential experiences of the commuter in south-east England: the tensions of town and country, stasis and movement, individuality and the crowd.

Parish of enormous hayfields
Perivale stood all alone,
And from Greenford scent of mayfields
Most enticingly was blown
Over market gardens tidy,
Taverns for the bona fide,
Cockney singers, cockney shooters,
Murray Poshes, Lupin Pooters
Long in Kensal Green and Highgate
silent under soot and stone.

From "**Middlesex**", *in* A Few Late Chrysanthemums *(1954)*

JG Ballard in the outlands

The suburbs dream of violence. Asleep in their drowsy villas, sheltered by benevolent shopping malls, they wait patiently for the nightmares that will wake them into a more passionate world…

Wishful thinking, I told myself as Heathrow airport shrank into the rear-view mirror, and more than a little foolish, an advertising man's ingrained habit of tasting the wrapper rather than the biscuit. But they were thoughts that were difficult to push aside. I steered the Jensen into the slow lane of the M4, and began to read the route signs welcoming me to the outer London suburbs. Ashford, Staines, Hillingdon – impossible destinations that featured only on the mental maps of desperate marketing men. Beyond Heathrow lay the empires of consumerism, and the mystery that obsessed me until the day I walked out of my agency for the last time. How to rouse a dormant people who had everything, who had bought the dreams that money can buy and knew they had found a bargain?

The indicator ticked at the dashboard, a nagging arrow that I was certain I had never selected. But a hundred yards ahead was a slip road that I had somehow known was waiting for me. I slowed and left the motorway, entering a green-banked culvert that curved in on itself, past a sign urging me to visit a new business park and conference centre. I braked sharply, thought of reversing back to the motorway, then gave up. Always let the road decide . . .

Like many central Londoners, I felt vaguely uneasy whenever I left the inner city and approached the suburban outlands. But in fact I had spent my advertising career in an eager courtship of the suburbs. Far from the jittery, synapse-testing metropolis, the perimeter towns dozing against the protective shoulder of the M25 were virtually an invention of the advertising industry, or so account executives like myself liked to think. The suburbs, we would all believe to our last gasp, were defined by the products we sold them, by the brands and trademarks and logos that alone defined their lives.

Yet somehow they resisted us, growing sleek and confident, the real centre of the nation, forever holding us at arm's length. Gazing out at the placid sea of bricky gables, at the pleasant parks and school playgrounds, I felt a pang of resentment, the same pain I remembered when my wife kissed me fondly, waved a little shyly from the door of our Chelsea apartment, and walked out on me for good. Affection could reveal itself in the most heartless moments.

But I had a special reason for feeling uneasy – only a few weeks earlier, these amiable suburbs had sat up and snarled, then sprung forward to kill my father.

From Kingdom Come *(2006)*

MY COMMUTE: THE MUSIC LOVER

Chris Parkin, The Oxford Tube: Oxford Thornhill Park & Ride to London Victoria Bus Station, February 2009–August 2012

Three days a week for nearly three years I was surrounded by a sea of slumber on the bus from Oxford to London. But I could never submit to heavy eyelids. It would've meant writing off that precious 90 minutes spent polishing off writers' entire works or scouring obscure music books and, when 3G permitted, unearthing the music within.

Most of these accumulated hours were spent compiling mazy, ever-changing soundtracks to complement the views and seasons outside. Winter was easy: something dark, glowering and difficult, to keep me on my toes.

Spring and summer required more thought. Bucolic daybreak music as the M40 cut a chalky path through Aston Rowant, a steep, heavily wooded Area of Outstanding Natural Beauty, and Watlington Hill, which has a chalk triangle on its slopes, said to have been placed there by local vicar Edward Horne, who was ashamed that his church lacked a spire.

A propulsive motorik sort of music was called for after Exit Five, before rappers, ravers and post-punks muscled in as we passed the conical hills of Northala Fields, built from the rubble of the old Wembley Stadium, and the CEO-ferrying planes at Northolt. Outside the airfield a Polish man, Paul Bonowicz, protested lonely against Winston Churchill's cover up of the Katyn Massacre. At this point Crass always seemed a good choice.

Only once did I suffer the dreaded six-hour crawl back to Oxford, thanks to an M40 pile-up. But while all around gnashed their teeth, I carried on selflessly scoring our journey.

Primrose Hill in the 1850s

…we reached a suburb of new houses, intermingled with wretched patches of waste land, half built over. Unfinished streets, unfinished crescents, unfinished squares, unfinished shops, unfinished gardens, surrounded us. At last they stopped at a new square, and rang the bell at one of the newest of the new houses. The door was opened, and she and her companion disappeared. The house was partly detached. It bore no number; but was distinguished as North Villa. The square – unfinished like everything else in the neighbourhood – was called Hollyoake Square.

I noticed nothing else about the place at that time. Its newness and desolateness of appearance revolted me, just then.…

From Basil *(1852) by Wilkie Collins*

West Horsley in the 1950s

"In the old days we had horse ploughs and there would be perhaps two men who looked after the horses, and there would be several men out working on the hedges while lots worked on the land. Well, there's still the same roads and lanes now, but much more has been put on them and lots more people live here. Up at the corner, where all the houses are, this was just one orchard belonging to the man across the road, and the kids used to go scrumping apples and pears there. Well, it changed because so many more people came to live here, and they were all such a busy kind. I mean, if they work in London they're out of the village all day so you don't really get to know them. In the old days you used to see men cycling to go up to work down the farm, but when the commuters came they just buzzed along in a car. The car absolutely ruined it: you didn't get to know people like you used to. We would say, 'Oh that's Mrs. Johnson, that's Mrs. Childs and that's Mrs. Hutchins.' But that's changed now and you don't get all the old friendliness."

Dorothy Harris, quoted in Humphries, Steve and Taylor, John, *The Making of Modern London 1945–85*

Old Hertfordshire

Plummers Park was thirty miles from Central London, in the latitude of Ruislip, in the country but not of it. The fields seemed almost touchable yet remote. Wild roses bloomed and blew in seclusion just out of reach; rooks and flashing magpies in elm and rowan were merely distant birds in distant trees; the fox and rabbit went unseen from the human windows. On Sundays the people had to drive out in their cars to witness a pig. The estate was the strangest crop ever to grow on the old Hertfordshire farming land.

From Tropic of Ruislip *(1974)*
by Leslie Thomas

Where town meets country

Garden Cities tend to make people think of anything but gardens. The names of Letchworth and Welwyn (the two originals), along with later incarnations such as Telford and Milton Keynes, probably suggest concrete piazzas, multi-storey car parks, drabness and high-density dwellings. All that, with a fast train to somewhere else.

Such was never the intention. The template for the Garden City was the brainchild of Ebenezer Howard, born in 1850 into a lower middle-class family in the City of London, the son of a Nonconformist shopkeeper. Schooled in Hertfordshire and Suffolk, he worked at a number of clerical jobs and also as a reporter during a stay in the US – where he read the works of Emerson and Whitman – before taking up the position of recorder at Hansard, proofreading the accounts of parliamentary debates and speeches.

Howard was sufficiently inspired by American author Edward Bellamy's best-selling fantasy *Looking Backward* (1888), about a socialist utopia, to pay out of his own pocket to have it published in England. He also read Henry George's 1879 treatise, *Progress and Poverty*, which examined the relationship between poverty and technology and the concentration of wealth in cities.

Though he never trained as a planner, designer or architect, Howard began to develop an idea for a society in which transport, people and places were arranged in such a way as to ensure optimum happiness and productivity for the greatest number of citizens. In his seminal *Garden Cities of Tomorrow* (1902), he proposed a new kind of semi-urban environment in which families were housed in low-rent homes in residential districts that were clean, airy, slum-free and close to the workplace.

Central to his concept was the image of the "Three Magnets", three forces or sets of attributes that characterise a particular place, namely "Town", "Country" and – his idealistic hybrid – the "Town-Country". As Howard explained, "Neither the Town magnet nor the Country magnet represent the full plan and purpose of nature. Human society and the beauty of nature are meant to be enjoyed together. As man and woman by their varied gifts and faculties supplement each other, so should town and country... I will undertake, then, to show how in 'Town-Country' equal, nay better, opportunities of social intercourse may be enjoyed than are enjoyed in any crowded city, while yet the beauties of nature may encompass and enfold each dweller therein; how higher wages are compatible with reduced rents and rates; how abundant opportunities for employment and bright prospects of advancement may be secured for all; how capital may be attracted and wealth created; how the most admirable sanitary conditions may be ensured; how beautiful homes and gardens may be seen on every hand; how the bounds of freedom may be widened, and yet all the best results of concert and co-operation gathered in by a happy people."

Howard's model city was laid out in a concentric pattern, with housing, industry and public parks arranged around radial thoroughfares. A glass arcade full of shops, called the "Crystal Palace", was to be functional but also a thing of beauty. Green space would

THE
THREE MAGNETS.

always be close at hand and varied entertainment venues would keep workers content. "Six magnificent boulevards," Howard tells us, "each 120 feet wide, traverse the city from centre to circumference, dividing it into six equal parts or wards. In the centre is a circular space containing about five and a half acres, laid out as a beautiful and well-watered garden; and, surrounding this garden, each standing in its own ample grounds, are the larger public buildings – town hall, principal concert and lecture hall, theatre, library, museum, picture-gallery, and hospital. The rest of the large space encircled by the 'Crystal Palace' is a public park, containing 145 acres, which includes ample recreation grounds within very easy access of all the people."

Howard joined forces with the William Morris-influenced urban planners Raymond Unwin and Richard Barry Parker, both fresh from designing the model village at Eastwick near York. They acquired land in Letchworth in Hertfordshire in 1903 and built the first homes – kitchenless units with a communal cooking and dining area – of the world's first so-called "Garden City" (though Howard had come across the motto *Urbs in Horto*, the "City in the Garden", during an earlier visit to Chicago). The construction of Letchworth's Spirella corset factory from 1912 fulfilled Howard's tenet that a Garden City should not merely be a dormitory town for London. In 1913, Howard moved into one of the Letchworth housing units.

Howard had envisaged several garden city satellites orbiting around the central mothership, all connected by a streamlined network of road and rail. In 1919, Welwyn was inaugurated as the second Garden City. In reality, however, both Letchworth (35 miles from London) and Welwyn (23 miles) have devolved into dormitory towns; the A1(M) motorway as well as frequent fast trains make both ideal commuter towns. The Spirella factory ceased production in 1989.

Yet though only two Garden Cities were built according to the original plan, many British New Towns are derived from the Letchworth model, while hyper-designed cities such as Brasilia – not to mention dozens of North American green-belt towns – incorporate key elements of Ebenezer Howard's pioneering vision.

To a Fat Lady Seen From the Train

O why do you walk through the fields
in gloves,

Missing so much and so much?

O fat white woman whom nobody loves,

Why do you walk through the fields
in gloves,

When the grass is soft as the breast
of doves

And shivering sweet to the touch?

O why do you walk through the fields
in gloves,

Missing so much and so much?

Frances Cornford (1910)

The Jesuit's hat

'Tis true that the suburbs of London are much larger than the body of the city, which make some compare her to a Jesuit's hat, whose brims are far larger than the block; which made count Gondomar the Spanish Ambassador himself to say, as the Queen of Spain was discussing with him, upon his return from England, of the City of London, "Madam I believe there will be no City left shortly, for it will have run out the gates to the suburbs!"
From Londonopolis *(1657) by James Howell*

THE CITY GENT: STRIPPED

3. THE BRIEFCASE

There is something very 1985 about the hard "executive" case, made from faux leather with metal edging, sporting a combination lock and containing within an accordion of inner flaps and perhaps a "writing board". An advertising blurb on the internet from the year 2013 promoting a leading case manufacturer's "hard ABS" update of this classic was still boasting about its product's "interior compartments for pens and computer diskettes". In the age of the tablet and e-reader, the freesheet and Pret, a big, heavy, bruise-inducing case seems superfluous, and even eccentric.

Lawyers, of course, still need to pack their briefs – though they often drag their Sisyphean burden around on a trolley. Accountants, too, have to freight huge amounts of paper. The popular doctor-ish cases they use are the direct descendants of the floppy medieval satchel – used for carrying money and valuables in the days before banks – and the French carpet bag. In the so-called creative industries, the floppy man's handbag ('manbag'), pioneered by Samuel Beckett, is *de rigueur* – though Dolce & Gabbana, Tom Ford and other brands flog £1000 versions of the same. Other firms have tried to cash in on the American TV series *Mad Men* and the evergreen James Bond franchise and re-packaged the hinged cases. Betjeman captured the snobbery of his own class and era when he wrote: "I am a young executive. No cuffs than mine are cleaner;/I have a Slimline brief-case and I use the firm's Cortina." Work, though, no longer fits neatly inside lockable cases, and a poet mocking an iPad user would seem ludicrously out of touch.

The Fat White Woman Speaks

Why do you rush through the fields in trains,

Guessing so much and so much?

Why do you flash through the flowery meads,

Fat-head poet that nobody reads;

And why do you know such a frightful lot

About people in gloves and such?

And how the devil can you be sure,

Guessing so much and so much,

How do you know but what someone who loves

Always to see me in nice white gloves

At the end of the field you are rushing by,

Is waiting for his Old Dutch?

GK Chesterton (c.1933)

Estate Agent's advert

for a three-bedroom, semi-detached house in South Ruislip.
April 2013. £385,000.

KITCHEN

Double aspect with two double glazed windows to the rear and door to side leading into the garden, part tiled walls providing splash back to a range of dark oak effect eye and base level units incorporating display units, wine racks, shelving and spice drawers, laminate work surfaces, inset one and a half bowl sink unit with mixer tap, fitted electric double oven and four ring gas hob with extractor canopy over, convector heater, space for upright fridge/freezer, ceramic tiled flooring, archway to;

UTILITY AREA

In praise of Suburbia

Suburbia, along with its exurban cousin, has become the greatest zone of growth – in loving, in working and in creative vigour. This comes about in the teeth of all attempts to divert such growth. We should welcome this as a thriving example of individual choice. Non-Plan is struggling through, against the odds. The supposed social ill-effects have been constantly exaggerated. The suburbs, even the exurbs, are a vital component of the city. The semis of Kenton or Bromley, the malls at Lakeside and Bluewater: these are as important to present-day London as Trafalgar Square or Pall Mall. They are far more important – whatever the architecture journals say – than the Modernists' Barbican or Roehampton high-rise flats. We have been trapped before in the argument for greater density. The quest always ends up being abandoned, leaving ruins behind. The difficulties of forcing people to live all too close to other people, when they would rather not, become all too apparent. Both Mayfield Avenue in Kenton, and Milton Keynes in Buckinghamshire, in their different ways demonstrate that suburbia is admirably flexible and adaptable. It is a blessedly anarchic form.

From The Freedoms of Suburbia *(2009) by Paul Barker*

Timeline III

Metropolitan Railway incorporated as the Bayswater, Paddington and Holborn Bridge Railway and granted powers to create an underground railway from Paddington to Farringdon

1853

Double decker bus (horse-drawn) invented in Paris

1853

Paris-based Anglo-French firm the Compagnie Générale des Omnibus is formed to buy up several operators in London; runs a competition to design a more spacious bus.

1855

Aylesbury and Buckingham Railway is incorporated; it opens eight years later, connecting the Metropolitan line to Vervey Junction

1860

North London Railway Act for the extension of railways between Dalton and Broad Street (on the edge of the city) requires one workmen's train to be run each way for a fare of 1d. Three years later it becomes normal practice for Parliament to require the promoters of all new lines through the built-up area of London to run workmen's trains

1861

Metropolitan Railways opens world's first 'cut and cover' underground railway between Paddington and Farringdon

10 January 1863

Cannon Street station opens

1866

Northern line, the first deep-level, electric 'tube' opens between Stockwell and King William Street Station in the City

November 1890

Metropolitan line
reaches Harrow

Cornflakes invented
by Kellogg´s

1880

1895

1893

1898

1899

Crompton, Stephen J.
Cook & Company sell an
electric toaster invented
by Scottish scientist Alan
MacMasters

Gladstone's coffin is
transported to his
funeral by tube

First bus to have a
petrol engine is run
by the Motor Traction
Company and runs
between Kensington
and Victoria

4

PLATFORM

The commuter is a classical hero, poised, his

plinth the smooth concrete of the railway platform.

Or perhaps he is an actor, touring from surburb to

terminus, repertory to West End; private and secretive

in the green room of the carriage but public,

hyper-conscious, on the platform.

I moved to Surbiton in 2003. I was ambiguous about the town and its name – Suburbiton, everyone says unfunnily – but loved the 1930s Art Deco-style station. It made me think of crematoria, power stations, old cinemas. The cold stone walls, intended to hide the chaos of human traffic, provided a suitable setting for a dawn ritual that could, for some, be life-long.

Upstairs, through the barrier, and then downstairs and then: the plaform. Here, the commuter is a classical hero, poised, his plinth the smooth concrete of the railway platform. Or perhaps he is an actor, touring from surburb to terminus, repertory to West End; private and secretive in the green room of the carriage but public, hyper-conscious, on the platform. Or he is a philosopher, learning how to wait and how to stare into space. Opposite is the empty platform: the side he might escape on one day. Between, an abyss, a suicide, a crude metaphor. Or he's a sportsman – it's a scrum out there at 7:53 and there's six minutes of jostling, conniving, plot-ting, pretending to text as he shuffles along Platform 2 to the precise spot where, any moment now, the left-side sliding door of carriage seven will glide to a standstill. He belongs, he's new to the commute, part of the throng, a member of a clan, learning the ropes, taking photos of himself. Or a time-worn loner, stranded at the rainy end of the long causeway just to get that standing place near the door at the end of the train where he can open his novel...

Platforms are like tombs, full of memories. My deepest are at Euston, the high numbers on the west or the low ones at the library end. I arrived on one of these years ago to live in London and then I used the same to commute home to family, a first love, funerals. My lightest train travels have begun in the same station, walking up, slightly tipsily, to the door of the cosy carriages of the Caledonian sleeper: Britain's last great rail adventure.

A commuter train, caught only once in life, could be as thrilling as a TGV to Marseilles or an ICE to Berlin. How

"A commuter train, caught only once in life, could be as thrilling as a TGV to Marseilles or an ICE to Berlin"

those European through-platforms dizzy the imagination with inter-continental possibility. But catch a train again and again and the relationship becomes automatic and mechanical. In some countries the word for commuter is *pendolare, pendelaar, pendlare*. In nineteenth-century England, the coming and going of passengers was known as "oscillation". The network is a huge clock, the pendulating passengers providing energy through friction. The departing platform is a penning-up, the arrival concourse a bursting forth.

The 8:08 always travels to Waterloo. So does the 8:23 and the 8:46 and every train that comes each quarter of an hour. The stops are all the same. Some of these services have been running, with only slight changes, for a century or more. The psychological state of the commuter is defined by repetition, habit and compulsion. It is on the platform that the caged life is felt most keenly. On the train there is at least the potential pleasure of vibration and motion, and the cinematic effect of the train windows – even if the view is always the same, the eye catches a different set of blurs each day.

The world of the commuter fans out from London; railway lines split and divide, reach out and stray. London is a cluster of termini, black dots where all paths end. There is always an exit to be found at the suburban platform, a way out of it all.

Somehow, the walk to the station can seem as if it's happening to someone else – clacking high heels, polished brogues, a swinging briefcase, a hat-tipping to the postman, garden gates clicking safely shut. In the early stages of the commuter's career, he may see himself as a TV star, under a sunny sky. But with time the walk becomes automatic, head down, just get there, don't waste time looking at your watch.

On the platform he is certain it is only happening to him. Heidegger uses the term "waitful" to describe the silent, sombre readiness of those who are lost in their thoughts and reflections. ■

This Train

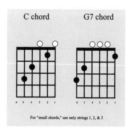

This train is bound for glory, this train.
This train is bound for glory, this train.
This train is bound for glory,
Don't carry nothing but the righteous and the holy.
This train is bound for glory, this train.

This train don't carry no gamblers, this train;
This train don't carry no gamblers, this train;
This train don't carry no gamblers,
Liars, thieves, nor big shot ramblers,
This train is bound for glory, this train.

This train don't carry no liars, this train;
This train don't carry no liars, this train;
This train don't carry no liars,
She's streamlined and a midnight flyer,
This train don't carry no liars, this train.

…This train don't carry no con men, this train;
This train don't carry no con men, this train;
This train don't carry no con men,
No wheeler dealers, here and gone men,
This train don't carry no con men, this train.

This train don't carry no rustlers, this train;
This train don't carry no rustlers, this train;
This train don't carry no rustlers,
Sidestreet walkers, two bit hustlers,
This train is bound for glory, this train.

Traditional (Anon.)

The Commuter Playlist

1. *Did You Ever Have a Dream?* David Bowie. Still being a Jones from Bromley is felt keenly in this 1967 B-side. "You can walk around in New York while you sleep in Penge," sounds like an acid-commute.

2. *Trans Europe Express*. Kraftwerk. Sometimes you need to believe. This 1977 album title track pays homage to epic commutes and is as smooth and seductive as a Synthanorma Sequenzer.

3. *Choo Choo Ch'Boogie*. Louis Jordan. 1946. Life is good. Commuting is fun. And "I love to hear the rhythm of the clickety clack."

4. *Up the Junction*. Squeeze. This 1979 hit song most obviously references the eponymous 1968 film; both turn on an unplanned pregnancy, neither ends well, but at least the song has a wonderfully happy melody.

5. *The Passenger*. Iggy Pop. Mr Osterberg's upbeat ubiquo-song about the flaneuring "riiiiide" of the transport-borne man at leisure. From 1977's "Lust for Life".

6. *Let's Submerge* by X-Ray Spex. Poly Styrene in finest form in 1978, inviting us to travel down in to the "subterrene" world of the Tube.

7. *Take the A Train*. The train-ride is a recurring theme for jazz and Billy Strayhorn's 1939 mellow jazz standard became Duke Ellington's signature tune.

8. *Down in the Tube Station at Midnight*. The Jam. 1978. "The wine will be flat and the curry's gone cold."

9. *Transport of Delight*. Flanders & Swann. 1956. Hold very tight please, on the "Big six-wheeler, scarlet-painted, London Transport, diesel-engined, ninety-seven–horse-power…omnibus!"

10. *9 to 5*. Sheena Easton. A very 1980, very happy hit song about the joys of work, with a video that features Easton cycling to catch a steam train, singing about her commuting "baby", buffing the boiler and pumping the valves to let off steam: "Night time is the right time, we make love."

11. *Baker Street*. Gerry Rafferty. This 1978 number one might be the sax-busker's tiresome serenade to the rushing, deep-pocketed commuter, but it has got great lyrics about urban anomie too.

12. *Sound of the Suburbs*. The Members. 1979. Camberley, Sunday – a catchy New Wave song by a band that never quite escaped the suburbs of minor success.

13. *Cars*. Gary Numan. 1979. The commuter's conundrum. You may feel safe and secure, but "nothing seems right in cars". Or planes, Gary, or planes.

14. *Londinium*. Catatonia. A 1999 Welsh lament for the hills: "My black cab rolls through the neon disease/Endlessly, endlessly/I come alive outside the M25."

15. *Metroland*. OMD. Recent but unashamedly lo-fi, retro ditty from the Scouse synthpoppers, from the 2013 album "English Electric", named after a Betjeman poem.

16. *You're On the Right Track Baby (But You're Heading the Wrong Way)*. Martha Davis and her Torrid Trio get to the heart of the commuter's dilemma in this swinging hit.

"*Commuter Love*" (1998)
The Divine Comedy

Freezing Monday morning
She is waiting for her train to come
I brush past her, smell her perfume
Watch her hair move as she turns to go
She doesn't know I exist
I'm gonna keep it like this
I'm not gonna take any risks this time
She's not like the others
With their papers and their headphones on

She reads novels by French authors with
loose morals
She can do no wrong
I wouldn't say I'm obsessed
I don't wanna see her undressed
We can be prince and princess in my dream
And we're dancing
Through the evening
'til the morning

Philosophical stances…

Waiting, like breathing, feeding and excreting is a primal state. The whole body seems to yawn when it waits. The Scholar, in Heidegger's *Country Path Conversations*, says, "Waiting has, properly speaking, no object." Another character in the same work, the Guide adds, "Waiting lets itself be involved in the open itself." And then the Scientist nods and remarks how, in searching for the right way to think, all three of them have become more "waitful".

FRIEDRICH NIETZSCHE ON PATIENCE

Weaknesses are being repackaged as virtues, there's no doubt about it…the impotence of the non-achiever becomes "kind-heartedness"; craven cowardice becomes "humility"; capitulation to those we detest is reinterpreted as "obedience"…The passivity of the weak – the pusillanimity with which they are so richly endowed, their timorous hovering-at-the-door approach, their gutless insistence on waiting – all this becomes "patience", moral probity itself; I-can't-stand-up-for-myself becomes I-refuse-to-take-revenge – "forgiveness" even ("for they know not what they do – only we know what they do!"). They also talk of "loving their enemies" – and break out into a sweat at the very words.
From On the Genealogy of Morals *(1887), trans. AB Barber*

SØREN KIERKEGAARD ON REPETITION

Repetition is a durable garment, true in its fit, neither too tight nor too baggy. Hope is a lovely young girl, who slithers away from your grasp; Memory is a lady of maturer years, never fully serving the purpose of the moment. Repetition is a beloved wife, of whom one never grows tired, for it is only of novelty that man wearies. One never grows tired of the familiar; and when one has it before one, one is happy.
From Repetition: A Venture in Experimental Psychology *(1843), trans. AB Barber*

MARTIN HEIDEGGER ON WAITING

Out of the experience of waiting, and indeed out of the experience of waiting upon the self-opening of the open-region, and in relation to such waiting, this waiting was spoken of, addressed [*angesprochen*], as releasement… Most of all we stand idle.
The Guide in *Country Path Conversations* (1966)

Mr. Weasley walks to work

"You don't normally walk to work, do you?" Harry asked him, as they set off briskly around the square.

"No, I usually Apparate," said Mr. Weasley, "but obviously you can't, and I think it's best we arrive in a thoroughly non-magical fashion...makes a better impression, given what you're being disciplined for..."

Mr. Weasley kept his hand inside his jacket as they walked. Harry knew it was clenched around his wand. The run-down streets were almost deserted, but when they arrived at the miserable little underground station they found it already full of early-morning commuters. As ever when he found himself in close proximity to Muggles going about their daily business, Mr. Weasley was hard put to contain his enthusiasm.

"Simply fabulous," he whispered, indicating the automatic ticket machines. "Wonderfully ingenious."

"They're out of order," said Harry, pointing at the sign.

"Yes, but even so..." said Mr. Weasley, beaming at them fondly.

They bought their tickets instead from a sleepy-looking guard (Harry handled the transaction, as Mr. Weasley was not very good with Muggle money) and five minutes later they were boarding an underground train that rattled them off towards the centre of London. Mr. Weasley kept anxiously checking and re-checking the Underground Map above the windows.

"Four more stops, Harry... Three stops left now... Two stops to go, Harry..."

They got off at a station in the very heart of London, and were swept from the train in a tide of besuited men and women carrying briefcases. Up the escalator they went, through the ticket barrier (Mr. Weasley delighted with the way the stile swallowed his ticket), and emerged on to a broad street lined with imposing-looking buildings and already full of traffic.

From Harry Potter and the Order of the Phoenix *(2003) by JK Rowling*

Waiting...

He who has waited long enough, will wait forever. And there comes the hour when nothing more can happen and nobody more can come and all is ended but the waiting that knows itself in vain.

From Malone Dies *(1956) by Samuel Beckett*

MY COMMUTE: THE DREAMER

Bob Greig, founder of onlydads.org, Thornton Heath to Victoria, 1988–1996

The commute offered two choices: wait for the next, hopefully less crowded train, or travel in the opposite direction to board at East Croydon for a faster train into town. I played once or twice, but generally adopted the grin-and-bear-it approach and got on the first train heading north.

It was a grind, commuting in on a sometimes ridiculously overcrowded train via Clapham Junction, looking out of the window; everything moving so fast. I was in my mid-twenties, doing a regimented office job and newly married. Life had become timetabled, lacking in alternatives, other lines of action. I'd gone from having no direction to commuting in just one.

The fast trains came through, non-stop, sending out a two-tone fanfare as they left us standing there looking in. You'd see people in first-class carriages, enjoying the space. It was a torment. When you commute, you catch people's eyes all the time. You wonder what jobs they do, where they're from. In London there are people from all over the world and you have no way of reading them.

I used to daydream – or dawn-dream – about moving up at work, perhaps having my own office instead of the open-plan office I was in, being given a secretary or an assistant who could do the job for me. I wanted to become a Londoner, tell the folks in Cardiff I commuted every day and was the real thing. But I also thought about moving out to, say, Purley, to a bigger house.

Sometimes I used to go in to London in the early evening or afternoon on a Saturday, for a pint or to go to a gallery. I was in different clothes, I'd look out of the window and it all felt so different. It was the same if I went in to work at the weekend to do some overtime. I'm not sure what it was, but it was like a guilty pleasure.

You become a trainspotter when you commute. I used to wonder if the trains from the south coast had priority, like the Concorde from New York landing at Heathrow. So I'd be on my packed stopping train, stuck in limbo, and a fast train would pass through and I'd imagine the driver radio-ing ahead: "I'm coming in from Eastbourne, it's the 7am, make way!"

The journey home found me standing on the windy, echoing concourse at Victoria with a hundred thousand others, occasionally lifting my head to stare at the Departure Board. The Gatwick Express would catch my eye – from Victoria, at that time, it was the only noteworthy journey on offer. A daily glimpse of a bigger world. But I stuck with the little one. Commuting can wear down your imagination and ambitions quicker than you realise.

I love trains, inter-cities, foreign trains, I went round Europe and India on them. But the commute, really, it wasn't a train journey, not for anyone, surely everyone hates it, except perhaps the workers who come in first class on the fast train from Purley.

THE CITY GENT – STRIPPED

4. THE UMBRELLA

"An Englishman walks in a pouring rain, swinging his closed umbrella like a walking-stick."
Ralph Waldo Emerson

The umbrella gets its name from *umbra*, the Latin word for shade, and started life as a parasol. In Egypt there are pictorial records of sunshades being used by people of status 3,000 years ago. Some scholars have sought to link the brolly with Nut, the Egyptian goddess of the sky, who was sometimes shown as an umbrella-like figure, arching her body over the earth. In African religions, the umbrella proper, because of its associations with rain, is sometimes a symbol of fertility. The Chinese have been using umbrellas and parasols for millennia and probably invented the first collapsible devices.

At the beginning of the Victorian era, umbrellas were made from wood or baleen, which was heavy and hard to fold. In the 1850s, Sheffield industrialist Samuel Fox developed the Paragon frame (sometimes called the Fox Frame) that employed U-shaped steel ribs. One of his assistants, William Hoyland, set up a competing firm and patented the "Flexus" frame, which uses spring stretchers to increase tension. The most expensive umbrellas featured handles made from exotic hardwoods or from

ivory. Just as, in Asia and Africa, parasols and umbrellas were – and still are – held by servants or slaves to symbolise the wealth or power of their masters, carriage umbrellas were carried by butlers to shield arriving guests at houses and hotels. James Smith, which still runs a famous umbrella emporium on New Oxford Street, supplied umbrellas to the likes of Gladstone and Lord Curzon from its Savile Row branch.

Between the World Wars it became fashionable for gentlemen to have a black umbrella with a silk or oiled cotton canopy and a crook handle – this survived into the early 1950s. But, as functionality replaced elegance, the telescopic umbrella, with its rust-proof and rot-proof nylon or PVC canopy, became popular.

In recent years, the umbrella has been condemned by some as an anti-social weapon, designed to poke out the eyes of the unprotected – already irate for being soaked to the skin – as they dash along narrow pavements or struggle out of Tube exits. Storm umbrellas – with tapered canopies – and brolly-hats have been tried as alternatives, with little success.

The umbrella is destined to go the way of the cane – a museum piece evoking an era when decorum, distinction and dryness mattered to people and when each Londoner had a claim on at least a metre's radius of empty space.

Faintheart in a Railway Train

At nine in the morning there passed a church,
At ten there passed me by the sea,
At twelve a town of smoke and smirch,
At two a forest of oak and birch,
    And then, on a platform, she:

A radiant stranger, who saw not me.
I queried, "Get out to her do I dare?"
But I kept my seat in my search for a plea,
And the wheels moved on. O could it but be
    That I had alighted there!

Thomas Hardy (1920)

Two examples of sadism

i. Morning at Didcot. 07:00 from Oxford pulls in. Passengers disembark to wait at another platform for a faster train to London. When they have entered subway, announcer proclaims that fast train has been cancelled. They all turn back. At same time 07:00 moves quietly off, leaving them neatly stranded.

ii. Evening, somewhere around Tilehurst. Weary commuters sleep, read, or stare blankly. Suddenly a buffet attendant, who clearly prides himself on being a bit of a one, flings open door at end of coach, shouting: "Anyone for Didcot or Swindon?". Sheepish hands go up. He takes a long look before declaring: "Well, you're on the right train, ha ha ha ha!".
From Notes from Overground *(1984) by Tiresias (aka Roger Green)*

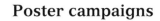

Poster campaigns

Take the Twopenny Tube and Avoid All Anxiety

Live in Kent and be Content

Live in Surrey, Far from Worry

The Sun Shines Most on the Southern Coast

A Good Move to Harrow Garden Village

So Swiftly Home by Southern Electric

Spend a day in Metro-land

THE "SILENT HIGHWAY"-MAN.
"Your MONEY or your LIFE!"

On that remarkable day, Saint James,

I undertook my Voyage down the Thames.

The Sign in Cancer, or the Ribs and Breast,

And Aeolus blew sweetly, West Southwest,

Then after many farewells, Cups and Glasses,

(Which oftentimes hath made men worse than asses)

About the waist or Navel of the Day,

Not being dry or Drunk, I went my way,

Our Wherry somewhat old, or struck in age,

That had endured near four years' Pilgrimage,

And carried honest people, Whores, and Thieves,

Some Sergeants, Bailiffs, and some under-Shrieves,

And now at last it was her lot to be

Th'adventurous bonny Bark to carry me.

From "A Very Merry Wherry Ferry Voyage" (1630) by John Taylor

Who pays the wherryman?

Dirty is Father Thames, I grant, thick, yellow, turbid,
occasionally evil-smelling; but I love him none the less.
From *The Business of Pleasure* (1879) by Edmund Yates

Until the middle of the eighteenth century there were only two bridges across the Thames: London Bridge and Putney Bridge. All points in between had to be forded by boat. Thames watermen plied a busy trade, rowing people, goods and animals across the river in wherries: small, swift rowing boats.

A wherry was either rowed by two oarsmen or propelled by a single man with a short paddle or "scull". Pamphleteer and poet John Taylor (1580–1653) was a sculler, making a living ferrying passengers along the Thames. He petitioned to prevent the theatre district from being moved north of the river as he depended on theatregoers for much of his income. Later members of the Company of Watermen would come to view the arrival of the hackney carriage with hostility and alarm.

Though their guild was held in public esteem, the Thames watermen were also known for their bellowing voices and bad language – despite byelaws prohibiting "immoderate, obscene and lewd expressions". For the 1717 premiere of his *Water Music*, Handel is said to have asked for a very loud performance in order to drown out the effing and blinding of the wherrymen.

Even after Westminster Bridge was completed, in 1750, the trip to Vauxhall Gardens was best made by boat because of thieves stalking the roads. Wherries were safe, functional and very fast. Pepys' contemporary, John Evelyn, notes in his diary: "I saw the rich Gudola sent his Majestie from the sate of Venice, but it was not comparable for swiftnesse to our common wherries."

Sewage, municipal regulations, strikes and the Blitz all contributed to the decline of the Thames as a thoroughfare for local traffic. The Tube and buses, and the eventual removal of the docks downriver, made the watermen's trade obsolete. However, London River Services, a division of Transport for London, now carries 2,000-plus commuters every day on its Thames Clippers between Putney and Blackfriars and North Greenwich to the London Eye, and ferries tourists between the two Tate galleries.

The Tube on the telly... and other fakes

BROAD STREET
This mainline station, demolished in 1985, never had an associated Tube station. However, in the TV spy drama *Spooks*, the mainline station has an Underground station which is the target of Irish terrorists.

CAIRO EAST
Becomes the background of the cover for the 1980 Madness single "Baggy Trousers".

CHARNHAM
Appears in the TV soap *Family Affairs*.

HOBBS END
Strange artefacts are found during the construction of this station, some-where near Knightsbridge, in the BBC television series *Quatermass and the Pit* (1958–9).

NEW BRIDGE
Features in one of the Tom Clancy's Rainbow Six PC Games; the station has ticket barriers and a cut-and-cover Tube line, but – evidencing its

American creators – has a waiting area and lacks London Underground decor.

VAUXHALL CROSS
James Bond and M meet at this "disused station" in *Die Another Day* (2002). Maps in the background show that the station is the next one along from Hyde Park Corner, and yet Bond enters the station through a staircase located on the south bank of the River Thames. The set is based on Aldwych, a genuine disused station on a branch off from the Piccadilly line.

TEMPLE
Appears in the 2013 Bond film *Skyfall*, but is shown as a deep tube and not a cut-and-cover stop; a train crashes through the floor here but is, mysteriously, carrying no passengers.

WALFORD EAST
This fake District Line station appears in the long-running soap *EastEnders*. Fictitious timetables show that it occupies the place of Bromley-by-Bow station.

In a Station of the Metro (1916)

The apparition of these faces in the crowd;

Petals on a wet, black bough.

Ezra Pound

THE 8.45

Freesheets

"The newspaper you are reading is rubbish"
Transport for London litter campaign, 2013

The future of newsprint: a mulch of paper and
autumn rain, shoe-soled into a corner of the third
carriage on the 8:02 from Shenfield. Yet, half an hour
earlier, catch the avid office worker, barging on to
stand firm, using birdman elbows to make space to
scan and scour, myopically, today's syndicated "fun"
story: a dolphin that plays with a cat, a three-year-old
Indian boy with a PhD, a house falling off a cliff
somewhere in the Third World, top ten things to eat,
do, drink, wear, read, hear, see, buy, buy.

CIRCULATIONS

DAILIES
Metro (London edition) 774,256
Standard 701,522
City A.M. 127,950

WEEKLIES
Shortlist 531,733
Stylist 433,482
Sport 302,466
Time Out 305,530

Oct–Dec 2012 figures. Source: Audit Bureau of Circulation

Railway time

Clocks became much more accurate in the eighteenth century because of mariners, who needed to know their precise longitude when crossing oceans. On land, the guards on horse-drawn coaches carried timepieces and adjusted these as they travelled, gaining perhaps 15 minutes over 24 hours as a coach travelled west to east (and losing the same for the return journey). Knowing the local "mean time" was sufficient while communications were slow.

In the early nineteenth century, with the advent of the railway, everything began to speed up. "Galvanic communication" (telegraphy by wires) became common and accurate timekeeping became a requirement, especially for those who worked on the railways, in the post office or in the telegraph offices. In London from the 1830s right up the 1940s, entrepreneurs such as John Henry Belville (timing assistant and meteorologist at the Royal Observatory at Greenwich) and his wife Maria and daughter Ruth (aka the Greenwich Time Lady) made a living commuting into and around London selling the right time to people.

In November 1840, a year after it had installed its first telegraph, the Great Western Railway ordered that London Time be used in all its timetables and at all its stations. This became known as Railway Time. On 17th February 1852, the installation of telegraph lines between the Greenwich Observatory and Lewisham Station was completed. By August, signals were sent on a regular basis from the Greenwich Observatory to London Bridge Station, too, and soon the scheme expanded. The correct time was telegraphed to stations at different times of the day and stationmasters were recommended to invite local watchmakers to adopt Greenwich Mean Time. In some towns outside the capital there was resistance, and some public clocks had two minute hands, one showing local, the other showing London time. In 1880, Parliament adopted GMT as the standard time for Great Britain.

Timeline IV

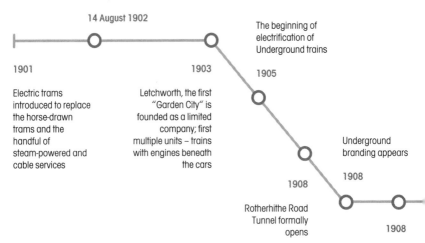

Opening of Greenwich Foot Tunnel beneath the Thames, connecting Greenwich to the Isle of Dogs

14 August 1902

The beginning of electrification of Underground trains

1901

1903

1905

Electric trams introduced to replace the horse-drawn trams and the handful of steam-powered and cable services

Letchworth, the first "Garden City" is founded as a limited company; first multiple units – trains with engines beneath the cars

Underground branding appears

1908

1908

Rotherhithe Road Tunnel formally opens

1908

First electric ticket-issuing machines

First escalators appear
in Earl's Court,
between District and
Piccadilly lines

1911

Pop-up toaster
patented by Charles
Strite in the United
States

1919

First trolleybuses
operate out of Fulwell

16 May 1931

1913

1924

Greater London Arterial
Roads Conference
approves the building of
255 miles of new roads
around the capital

Marie Cordery
becomes the first
baby born on the
Tube at Elephant and
Castle on the
Bakerloo line

5

IN

"Why do you do this everyday of the week wasting your life?

Well it's me job. And how long have you been doing it?

14 years. What is it all for? What's the purpose of it all?

What are we doing it for? Where are we going?

Where are we going?!"

"Waterloo!"

Commute has the same root as mutate: to change, to be transformed. The journey into work is a transformative event, as we change not only place but also personality. We are alone, in the midst of millions. We are unfettered by domestic or occupational demands. We are, for a moment, free from the obligation to control our destiny; public transport allows movement without responsibility. We could be anyone, we could run away.

"Train travel is a film for which we haven't bought a ticket," writes Iain Sinclair in *London Orbital*, which narrates his high-minded hike through the capital's commuter zones. The context is the reverse commute, heading back into London at a time of day when everybody else is hurtling away from the city. But I have had such commutes on the way in. I have sought a space by a window and gazed out, the trick not to seek novelty in the unknown, but to let your eyes linger on the familiar and search for details.

Riding in from the south-west edges of London, you see, and feel, London gather around you. The punctuation marks of the stations come more frequently, the woods thin out and then you pass the spaces that denote a conurbation – a park, a race course, a shopping centre, a supermarket, an immense cemetery – and finally Clapham Junction sucks you in and spits you out into an inner city. Like all railway lines, this one sneaks in behind the houses, passing through, and above, untidy corners and hidden crevices. There is a speeding up then the slow taxi through the offices and terraces of Lambeth, parliament visible between glass towers. The window-flicker of reality is never dull.

It is not only about looking outwards. There is an inward movement. As regular commuters, we learn quickly how to screen out everything around us, ignore intimacy – glances, shared kisses, perfumes – and focus downwards. People on trains and Tubes and buses look down at their feet, a metaphor for the private navel-gazing they are engaging in. Alain de Botton describes entering a carriage as akin to "interrupting a congregation".

The reading today will be the freesheet. You'd have to be a neurotic to attempt to scope the hectic fraternity of a packed mass-transit carriage. Reginald Perrin, the middle-manager who travels every day from Norbiton to his office at Sunshine Desserts in the novels of David Nobbs (and in Nobbs's television adaptations of the same), tries just that. "Pompous fool. Look at all the blackheads all over his nose," he mutters to himself. His next line, "Is there any point in doing the crossword properly?" shouldn't be taken at face value. Every day, on every commute, Reggie Perrin has a minor existential crisis.

We move home and build up our London in fragments, and these are determined by journeys. I used the Piccadilly line for a year from Manor House to Holborn; I remember the gusting winds that assaulted you as you left at the suburban end. The Northern Line from Tooting Bec was an earlier year, and the journey was

"People on trains and tubes and buses look down at their feet, a metaphor for the private navel-gazing they are engaging in"

long and blind – it's typical of this fragmentary experience that you go underground a few metres from your favourite cheap curry caff and re-emerge next to one of Europe's best-known gay discos on a street from the Monopoly game. I used the Jubilee line for a longer period, from Waterloo to Canary Wharf, a ride through a more spacious, grey underworld to arrive at a cavernous, hubristic station. This last journey involved me using the No. 68 from Herne Hill, a bus I knew from more than 15 years earlier, still slow and favoured by the poor. Sometimes I ended up on the DLR, a toy train in a part of London where play, and children, were banned. For one year I walked into London, and began to join things up.

In my early twenties, before I worked every day, I looked up to what I thought of as the real commuters, the ones who come in from Basingstoke and Portsmouth. Their trains looked heavier, more purposeful, some even had engines up front. I think I imagined that a long commute was like a journey on an inter-city train, after which you alighted imbued with a spirit of discovery and adventure. But I know now that these long-serving commuters are the same as the rest of us, hunkered down behind their newspapers as they ride, every day, "up" to London, whatever that means.

One of the most often-quoted half-sentences about commuting is this, from"East Coker", one of TS Eliot's *Four Quartets* (1944):

Or as, when an underground train, in
  the tube, stops too long between
  stations
And the conversation rises and slowly
  fades into silence
And you see behind every face the
  mental emptiness deepen
Leaving only the growing terror of
  nothing to think about...

It's cruel, condescending, of its time, ponderously "poetic". But what if it is simply wrong? A commuter train is a train full of lives, hopes, fears, memories, thoughts. Behind every face is a mind that won't be lost amid the seeming mass of the anonymous. Even on the repeated commute, languor never quite sets in. There's time as you travel to revisit childhoods in provincial towns, lost journeys, recall rides on your bike, on single-carriage sprinters in East Yorkshire, on empty buses in rural south Wales, on diesel trains in Merseyside, on long, slow and sleepy lines up into the Highlands. How it might have been, to have fallen in love and got a job in another town, to be commuting on different trains to Leeds, Norwich, Exeter, Stirling, Carlisle, Mold. And London is the most international city in the world. The Brazilian commuter remembers the balsa-raft he used every day. The Beijinger once peddled through the hutongs. The Midwesterner used his dad's old car. A million unspoken memories flit around the morning's seeming sameness. That rich, many-tracked journey is internal, and endless.

The commuter of 2013, 2014, 2015 is multicultural, bus-using, bike-riding, zone-hopping. He is from all classes, from all walks of life, from boroughs that are not always quaintly suburban in the leafy – also dated – sense of that word. So it is curious how "culture" and the mass media still likes to view this universe through the eyes of Eliot and Betjeman and even Ballard (born 1930).

The enduring caricature of the commuter as invisible man may have its origins in the influential writings of Walter Benjamin, the German literary critic who translated the poems of Charles Baudelaire and used the French writer as a prism through which to analyse society and capitalism. His unfinished *Arcades Project* was to be a great encyclopaedia of Paris's built environment, its railway stations, shops and exhibition spaces rendered as "residues of a dream world". Gail Cunningham, in *London Eyes: Reflections in Text and Image*, sums up where the commuter might fit into this paradigm:

"The predominant terms for understanding the modern city largely rests on notions of alienation, disconnection and anonymity, with the flâneur, from Baudelaire through Benjamin and onwards, as the privileged representative of urban modernity. The commuter, I would argue, provides not only an equally significant but also a more empirically grounded alternative figure through which to apprehend the relations between individual and city, the personal and the mass."

It is, perhaps, time to come away from the lulling arcades and attempt a new definition." Cunningham's emphasis is on the hermeneutics of the commuter: how the gaze of the travelling worker might serve "culture" as a means by which to take in the city as an interconnected whole. This is only half way to a new commuter. How about championing the commuter as complete poet? As much as any nineteenth century Parisian drifter, a twenty-first century commuter can also be a rebel, a traveller, a thinker, a dreamer and a superhero, even if he's "grounded". The commuter, during the daily passage from home to work, acts out a metamorphosis worthy of Ovid or Chaucer. His heartbeat and pulse alter, his synapses reconfigure their firing patterns, his muscles tense up. To the iambs of the train upon the track, he lives out a narrative of his own. He doesn't merely see the city, he is the city.

Since 1900, since 1950, since 1970, the commuter has changed – and he changes every day ∎

Mr. Phillips finds a seat

Like most experienced commuters, Mr. Phillips has a variety of techniques for seizing somewhere to sit, sneaking in around the side of the door and sliding into one of the jump-seats or barrelling down to the far end of the compartment, through the thickets of passengers, briefcases, newspapers, outstretched legs... the battle for a space prepared you for, was an allegory or image of, the daily struggle... to them that hath shall be given, that was the deal.
From Mr. Phillips *(2003) by John Lanchester*

Dream house of the collective

Arcades, winter gardens, panoramas, factories, wax museums, casinos, railroad stations... Arcades are houses or passages having no outside – like the dream.
From The Arcades Project *(1927–40), by Walter Benjamin*

Patrick Hamilton and the London air

London, the crouching monster, like every other monster has to breathe, and breathe it does in its own obscure, malignant way. Its vital oxygen is composed of suburban working men and women of all kinds, who every morning are sucked up through an infinitely complicated respiratory apparatus of trains and termini into the mighty congested lungs, held there for a number of hours, and then, in the evening, exhaled violently through the same channels.

From The Slaves of Solitude *(2007)*

Moving movies

Films about commuting – and escaping from it

1. SLIDING DOORS (1998)
Former PR girl Helen Quilley (Gwyneth Paltrow) lives two very different parallel lives, each determined only by the boarding – or not – of a Tube train.

2. FIVE EASY PIECES (1970)
Stuck in a traffic jam, Bobby Dupea (Jack Nicholson) leaps out of his car and plays Chopin's *Fantaisie in F minor* on an old upright piano on the bed of a truck; the commuters' horns provide the woodwind.

3. ON THE BUSES (1971)
First of three films about cheeky Stan, his sister Olive and her husband Arthur, and toothbrush-moustachioed Blakey, and the joys and pains of life at Wood Green bus garage.

4. BRIEF ENCOUNTER (1945)
Repressed desire, fuzzy romance, a Noel Coward script, Rachmaninov's *Piano Concerto No. 2*, steam trains and "I wish you were dead! No, I don't, that's silly." Just another rail journey.

5. THE KNOWLEDGE (1979)
Who needs De Niro when you have this film about four men attempting to qualify as London taxi drivers and learning that the exam, well, it's just a metaphor, guv?

"I need some space"

Research into personal space suggests we humans are happiest when people stay outside a radius of between arm's length and four feet. The former would be fine for a Latin American or an Italian; the latter would be on the verge of intrusion for a certain kind of Englishman.

Congestion defines the London commuting experience. There is crowding at the doors of the suburban station, at the bus-stop, at the traffic lights on the bike path. There is cramming and ramming during the journey ("Move right down inside the cars!"). There is the squeeze to find the door, and get off ("Mind the Gap!"). And then the regimented movement from the train up escalators ("Stand on the right!") or into lifts built for an age when trains emptied by dozens rather than hundreds. Then there is the street anarchy, the queues for coffee or while picking up an early lunch – to beat the lunchtime queue later on in the day…

But the railways and the buses and the roads were introduced to ease congestion. In 1867, 3.5 million of the 8 million passengers using the recently opened terminus at Cannon Street were not going out to the suburbs; they were merely going down to London Bridge to catch another train to Charing Cross in the West End. That's a distance of less than two miles and they knew it was advisable to use the train.

In the nineteenth century, Benjamin Ball, a student of Charcot, defined claustrophobia as a fear of losing the option of escape and the control of one's actions – and one's sphincters – while being in a mass of people. Freud suggested the

anxiety felt was a projection of an unconscious conflict, possibly unused libido. Otto Fenichel claimed "claustrophobias...are often specially directed against fantasies of being in the mother's womb" and that the urge to escape from, say, a packed train was due in part to the movement, which induces an "increasing sexual excitement approaching orgasm".

Visitors to London often comment on the rudeness or brusqueness of its residents. But it's widely recognised that seeming anti-social behaviour is a defence mechanism for those who have to live among crowds. In his *The Pleasures and Sorrows of Work* (2009), Alain de Botton sees a kindness in the tacit agreement by commuters to keep silent "rather than revealing the extent to which they are covertly evaluating, judging, condemning and desiring each other".

American anthropologist Edward T Hall, who invented the science of Proxemics in the 1960s, defined four distances: intimate (6–18 inches); personal (1½–4 feet); social distance (4–12 feet) and public (12–25 feet). Most peak-time London commutes fall into the intimate category, and even those seated often have genitalia or buttocks inside the 18-inch radius. Environmental psychologist Robert Sommer, in *Personal Space: The Behavioral Basis of Design* (1969), considers how personal space differs from "territory" in that we carry it around with us. He also notes how we learn to apprehend fellow passengers as inanimate objects – if they accidentally touch us, we ignore it. This is, he says, a form of dehumanisation. The commuter, who has to survive the onslaught of adverts, announcements, barriers, buildings and, yes, fellow commuters, occupies a near-abstract world where all the usual rules are suspended. Far from being a flâneur, all gaze and gay *dérive*, he is compelled to live the journey as might a mystic or a monk.

Derrida on Kant on human rights

All human creatures, all finite beings endowed with reason, have received, in equal proportion, "common possession of the surface of the earth". No one can in principle, therefore, legitimately appropriate for himself the aforementioned surface (as such, as a surface-area) and withhold access to another man.
From On Cosmopolitanism and Forgiveness *(1997), by Jacques Derrida, trans. Mark Dooley*

The walking classes

During the nineteenth centry, London was around six miles wide and four miles from north to south. Almost 70 per cent of commuters went to work on foot in the City, not least because it was as fast as horses – carts and coaches moved at no more than four miles an hour through the narrow streets. Even when trains became available, fares were high, and as roads were paved, provided with drainage and – from the 1830s – given street lighting, walking became easier. The introduction of a police force in 1829 deterred muggers. Even as late as 1897 a quarter of London trade union members chose not to use the train.

MOVEMENT INTO AND OUT OF THE CITY (1854)

Omnibus passengers	88,000	15%
Steamer passengers	30,000	5%
Rail passengers via Fenchurch St. or London Br.	54,000	9%
Met passengers	8,440	1%
Walkers	400,000	69%

End of the road

The numbers behind London's jams

Vehicles registered: **2.5 million**

Increase in road traffic from 2003 to 2013: **20%**

Number of major roads built since 1989: **one (the M11)**

Busiest non-motorway road in the UK: **A3 Kingston bypass between Tolworth and New Malden (125,000 vehicles per day)**

Miles of roads: **9,000**

Miles of parking-free "red routes": **360**

Number of road tunnels: **13**

Number of sets of traffic lights: **6,000**

Average speed on roads: **9mph (same as in 1890)**

Slowest "rush hour" of the week: **4–5pm Friday**

Number of hours per year spent in a traffic jam: **66**

Congestion charge per day: **£10**

Most polluted road: **North Circular near Walthamstow**

Council earning most from parking charges: **Westminster, £38m (2011–12)**

24 hours' parking at Heathrow's short-stay car parks: **£53.90**

Three longest roads

A1 from St Paul's Cathedral to Edinburgh
A4 from Fleet Street to Bristol
A40 from High Holborn to Fishguard, Wales

Accidents

A breakdown of the 29,257 casualties recorded in 2011

159 fatalities
2,646 serious injuries
26,452 slight injuries

Sources: Transport for London; London Councils; BBC; INRIX; Clean Air in London

Very brief encounters

On the 7th March 2012, the *Daily Mail* reported the case of a man taken to court for "strumming an imaginary banjo on the train". A woman complained of seeing a newspaper moving on his lap as he breathed heavily on the 7:08am Basingstoke to Reading service. In court, the man said he was adjusting his underwear, adding "For my sins I play the banjo, so sometimes I do, with my hands, pick out a pattern on my knees." He was acquitted.

The commute is full of sexual possibility, from glad eyes to knocking knees to all manner of unavoidable intimacies. Frotteurism (rubbing of the groin against a non-consensual other) and toucherism (doing the same with a hand) break the rules of decorum, as well as the law. Frotteurs can now be caught on phone-cameras, which could, of course, encourage them.

Among the many other new "genres" of entertainment created by the mobile phone are the upskirt shots and videos snapped on trains and tubes. In Japan, famous for its crowded trains as well as its pervy predilections, *chikan* is the act of sexual assault by groping on public transport. It has spawned countless Anime and Manga strips showing women avoiding *chikan* perpetrators as well as *hentai* porn cartoons showing young schoolgirls enjoying hardcore *chikan* acts. Since 2006, Japanese subway trains have women-only cars and undercover police patrols look out for male offenders, and the less common female *chijo*. India, Indonesia, Taiwan, Egypt, Brazil and Mexico all have women-only buses or train carriages.

Freud rides the railroad

The shaking sensation experienced in wagons and railroad trains exerts such a fascinating influence on older children, that all boys, at least at one time in their lives, want to become conductors and drivers. They are wont to ascribe to railroad activities an extraordinary and mysterious interest, and during the age of phantastic activity (shortly before puberty) they utilise these as a nucleus for exquisite sexual symbolisms. The desire to connect railroad travelling with sexuality apparently originates from the pleasurable character of the sensation of motion.

From Three Contributions to the Sexual Theory *(1910) by Sigmund Freud, trans. AA Brill*

Happiness: the greatest thing that I possess

In the last decade, the science of "happiness studies" has grown and grown, producing the surveys and lists that the mass media loves. Among the headline-grabbing conclusions on commuting are the discoveries that:

TEN MINUTES' COMMUTE CUTS YOUR SOCIAL LIFE BY TEN PER CENT

COMMUTING TIME HAS A DETRIMENTAL EFFECT ON WOMEN'S PSYCHOLOGICAL HEALTH BUT NOT ON MEN'S

LONG-DISTANCE COMMUTERS ARE FOUND TO EXPERIENCE MORE STRESS AND OTHER NEGATIVE EFFECTS SUCH AS HIGHER BLOOD PRESSURE AND TROUBLE SLEEPING

A COMMUTE LONGER THAN 45 MINUTES FOR JUST ONE PARTNER IN A MARRIAGE MAKES THE COUPLE 40 PER CENT MORE LIKELY TO DIVORCE

EACH MINUTE YOU COMMUTE IS ASSOCIATED WITH A 0.0257-MINUTE EXERCISE TIME REDUCTION, A 0.0387-MINUTE FOOD PREPARATION TIME REDUCTION, AND A 0.2205-MINUTE SLEEP TIME REDUCTION

LONG COMMUTES CAUSE OBESITY, NECK PAIN, LONELINESS, DIVORCE, STRESS AND INSOMNIA

40 PER CENT OF EMPLOYEES WHO SPEND MORE THAN 90 MINUTES GETTING HOME FROM WORK EXPERIENCED WORRY FOR MUCH OF THE PREVIOUS DAY

A lot of interest, and speculation, was prompted by a paper by Swiss economists Bruno Frey and Alois Stutzer titled *The Stress that Doesn't Pay: The Commuting Paradox*, originally published in 2004. While never quite getting beyond a tentative case, the main point the Swiss happiness theorists make is that commuting breaks the widely accepted notion of "equilibrium". We are generally content to accept inconveniences – an office with no sunlight, a long and busy day's work, rudeness from our workmates – because of the returns, be they a decent salary, a nice house or a new car. But commuting, they say, breaks the rule: "People with longer commuting time report systematically lower subjective well-being." So a commuter who travels one hour, one way, would have to make 40 per cent more than his current salary to be as fully satisfied with his life as a non-commuter. He is miles away from anything like equilibrium. People usually overestimate the value of the things they'll obtain by commuting – more money, more material goods, more prestige – and underestimate what they are losing: social connections, hobbies, and health.

Seven canny commutes

ELEPHANT & CASTLE
As the obelisk at St George's Circus proudly announces, this area is one mile from Fleet Street, the City and Westminster (Palace Yard). It is, say locals, "the real centre of London". With some affordable housing, lots of history and a degree of gentrification, this neighbourhood – at the right end of snarled Walworth Road – is good for walkers, cyclists, train-takers and tubers and just 20 minutes on foot to the Thames.

HACKNEY
If you live around London Fields, you have a towpath all the way to Islington, ideal for cycling (25 minutes) or walking (an hour) the four and a bit miles to the City or West End.

HAMPSTEAD
Starting on a hill seems to speed things up by bus or car. The No. 46 bus, which runs along a huge upside-down V between the City, Swiss Cottage and the West End, can do the trip down to Lancaster Gate in 28 minutes or down to Holborn Circus in 38 minutes.

SURBITON
Fifteen miles from London, this suburb got its first station in 1838 because the oligopoly of Kingston coachmen refused to have one in their 'hood. It is "closer" in time (17 minutes is the fastest) to London than many inner boroughs. Houses here are considerably cheaper than in Richmond or Wimbledon. Other peripheral towns that are the last stop before London are: East Croydon (13 minutes to London Bridge), Watford Junction (15 minutes to Euston) and Reading (27 minutes to Paddington).

WEST HARROW & NORTH HARROW
These residential stations benefit from the fast Met line trains from Harrow on the Hill. From either, you can get to Baker Street in a smooth 24 minutes (Aldgate is 42–3 minutes, no changes).

RODING VALLEY
This Central Line stop in Essex processes just 210,000 passengers a year, making it the underground network's quietest station (Waterloo Tube has 82 million). It's 30 minutes to Bank, with a change at Woodford; 41 minutes if you want to do it on the same train, along the loop via Hainault.

ASHFORD INTERNATIONAL, KENT
Travel at 186 mph from Ashford in Kent to arrive 36 minutes – or almost 60 miles – later at St Pancras International, with just one short stop in Stratford.

THE CITY GENT: STRIPPED

5. THE PIN-STRIPE

The pin-stripe has a colourful, even chequered, past. Its simple, elegant pattern may derive from 1890s boating suits or military uniforms or be a natural extension of the striped trousers traditionally worn with a morning coat by City bankers. Fashion historians are divided as to whether the stripes are an example of flashy flamboyance or a continuation of the schoolboy's habit of wearing a uniform. This ambiguity might explain the popularity of the pinstripe with gangsters, English "Spivs", Hollywood actors – and lawyers. The pinstripe symbolises an attempt to legitimise something dubious or corrupt.

Churchill had several pinstripe suits. He wore his so-called "siren suit", which he designed himself, for long working nights during the air raids of World War II. In 2002 the suit fetched nearly £32,500 when it was sold at auction.

Dark enough to look sober, the narrow white lines purport to signify both straightness – of character and morality – and a hint of brightness and boldness. The lines, woven into worsted cloth, are made up of pinhead-sized dots of yarn in silk, mercerised cotton or man-made materials. The thicker chalk stripe is popular with senior barristers. The pin-stripe blazer is worn by many middle-aged men with jeans to suggest, in the words of one female comedian, "business up top, fun below".

Twenty productive commutes

1. Learn a language: repeat after me *"Io sono un pendolare felice"*.

2. Meditate: eyes closed, forget the world, use the dum-der-dum of the train.

3. Read the Booker books, the Pulitzer prizes, the Nobel novels.

4. Write the Booker books…

5. Draw or doodle: all those faces!

6. Exercise, secretly.

7. Do all your day's texting and tweeting – and then switch off till the next commute.

8. Memorise poems/stories.

9. Play I-Spy without the letters T, P or C.

10. Catch up on sleep.

11. Make new resolutions – edit existing ones.

12. Spot trains. Is that a class 458 Juniper or the Desiro 450?

13. Reinvent yourself (every day).

14. Pose.

15. Seduce someone.

16. Know thyself through aphorisms – read Socrates, Kierkegaard, Nietzsche, instead of the freesheets.

17. Crosswords – a commuter classic.

18. Listen to new genres of music (nose flutes, klezmer, Finnish tango) considerately.

19. Pray.

20. Read on…

Southern Electric!

During World War I, the emphasis was on co-ordinating railway services rather than competing. The government's Railway Executive Committee, set up in 1912, managed the lines mainly to move troops around and to impose economies on manpower, fuel and materials. Only a few lines were damaged in air-raids, but profits bombed.

With the end of the war, the need to improve and expand the lines returned. The government of Lloyd George resisted calls for nationalisation and decided, instead, to turn the 120 mainline companies into four big operators. The so-called "grouping" took place in 1923.

The trains to the suburbs on the north, west and east of London fell under the control of companies whose interests went far beyond the south-east, but Southern Railway, the smallest of the "Big Four", managed 2,186 miles (3,518 km) of lines that in the main fanned out from the capital. Where the others were predominantly freight operators, the Southern, despite its small size, carried more than a quarter of the UK's total passenger traffic.

Alert to the lucrative potential of the heavily trafficked commuter lines around London and also to the challenge from fast electric trams, the company, under the clear-headed leadership of Sir Herbert Ashcombe Walker, pursued a vigorous policy of electrification. By 1930, Southern operated 800 miles of electric track, amounting to 300 route miles. In 1931 work began on the UK's first electric main line, to Brighton, going on to operate six trains every hour and covering the 50 miles inside an hour.

With its Night Ferry trains to the continent, its "Belle" series of all-Pullman leisure trains – to Brighton, Bournemouth, Kent and Devon – and its eye-catching, Art Deco-influenced poster campaigns promoting the "sunny" south-east, the Southern added a dash of glamour to commuting and to rail travel in general. In the inter-war years, it grew to become the biggest urban electric railway network in the world and turned a healthy profit.

The General Strike, World War II – in which the Southern played a vital role embarking the British Expeditionary Force for the Dunkirk landings – and the rise of the motor-car heralded the end of the Southern's golden age. In 1947 the railways were nationalised. In 2008 Ashcombe Walker was voted "greatest railwayman of all time" by the readers of *Modern Railways* magazine.

Reading

Such an expression of unhappiness was enough by itself to make one's eyes slide above the paper's edge to the poor woman's face – insignificant without that look, almost a symbol of human destiny with it. Life's what you see in people's eyes; life's what they learn, and, having learnt it, never, though they seek to hide it, cease to be aware of – what? That life's like that, it seems.

Five faces opposite – five mature faces – and the knowledge in each face. Strange, though, how people want to conceal it! Marks of reticence are on all those faces: lips shut, eyes shaded, each one of the five doing something to hide or stultify his knowledge. One smokes; another reads; a third checks entries in a pocket book; a fourth stares at the map of the line framed opposite; and the fifth – the terrible thing about the fifth is that she does nothing at all. She looks at life. Ah, but my poor, unfortunate woman, do play the game – do, for all our sakes, conceal it!

As if she heard me, she looked up, shifted slightly in her seat and sighed. She seemed to apologise and at the same time to say to me, "If only you knew!" Then she looked at life again. "But I do know," I answered silently, glancing at the *Times* for manners' sake. "I know the whole business. 'Peace between Germany and the Allied Powers was yesterday officially ushered in at Paris – Signor Nitti, the Italian Prime Minister – a passenger train at Doncaster was in collision with a goods train…' We all know – the *Times* knows – but we pretend we don't." My eyes had once more crept over the paper's rim. She shuddered, twitched her arm queerly to the middle of her back and shook her head. Again I dipped into my great reservoir of life. "Take what you like," I continued, "births, deaths, marriages, Court Circular, the habits of birds, Leonardo da Vinci, the Sandhills murder, high wages and the cost of living – oh, take what you like," I repeated, "it's all in the *Times*!"
From An Unwritten Novel *(1920) by Virginia Woolf*

How to use a car park
"The true temples of the automobile age" JG Ballard

Gibson Road, Sutton: pornographic film set
Great Eastern Street: fashion catwalk
Smithfield Market: MI6 hideout in 2012 Bond film *Skyfall*
Peckham Rye: rooftop Campari bar and art centre
Moxon Street, Marylebone: farmers' market

Where are we going?

"And then there's me…a Charlie. You're just the same as they are. Have a look at yourself. Go on, have a look at yourself! Depressing isn't it? Same hat as them, same coat as them, same trousers, same papers, same sort of job…if it wasn't for the initials on your briefcase you wouldn't know who you were. It's too late for them to change they're in a rut, they'll go up to heaven on the 8:22 they will, but you're different! Why do you do this everyday of the week, wasting your life? Well it's me job. And how long have you been doing it? Fourteen years. What is it all for? What's the purpose of it all? What are we doing it for? Where are we going? Where are we going?!"

"Waterloo!"

Tony Hancock, from The Rebel *(1961), written by Ray Galton and Alan Simpson*

2012 busiest services

OPERATOR SERVICE LOAD FACTOR – which translated means how many people are on the train. 100% means packed to the hilt.

1. FGW 7:44am Henley-on-Thames to London Paddington **180%**

2. SWT 7:32am Woking to London Waterloo **164%**

3. LM 6:13pm London Euston to Birmingham New Street **162%**

4. LM 4:48pm Euston to Birmingham New Street **160%**

5. FGW 6:30am Banbury to Paddington **158%**

6. LM 7:55am Stourbridge Junction to Stratford-upon-Avon **157%**

7. FTP 6:23am Manchester Airport to Middlesbrough **155%**

8. NE 6:17pm London Liverpool Street to Shenfield **154%**

9. LM 7:14pm Alton to Waterloo **152%**

10. LM 5:46pm Euston to Birmingham New Street **152%**

MY COMMUTE: THE GENTLE CYCLIST

Brian Daughton, 51, teacher and photographer, Elephant & Castle to
Holloway Road, 2002–present

I don't dress as a navy seal. I'm not your classic urban cyclist. I go across Southwark Bridge – it's quiet and as bridges go it has a low profile. I'm told the fire services need it to be that way. Blackfriars Bridge would be more direct but it's busy.

I go by bike because it is less stressful than Tube or bus and if I leave home by a quarter past nine I can be giving a class around forty minutes later, easily. I'm sure the hardcore urban riders can get there in 20 minutes but I'm a laid back, easygoing cyclist. I take the scenic route: I go past the Guildhall – there are sometimes things going on but I'm on my way to work – and through the central arch at Smithfields. You're supposed to dismount but if there's no guard there I cycle through.

Sometimes, if I have time, I stop at Pret à Manger for a coffee or I buy some meat for a special occasion – there's a guy, at Abrahams, and he closes at 9, but he sells Argentine, Australian and Irish beef and I might buy something. He stays open later than most of the others. I pay him in cash. He doesn't take cards.

On London Road I see the London Wall – I see Roman and Medieval London on the way to work. After that I take a little left and go through an arch and go past the headquarters of St John Ambulance and then I go through Clerkenwell Green. I pass the Modern Pantry, a café-restaurant

and see all the media types having their "power breakfasts" and I always think "It'd be nice to stop here, one day I'll stop here", but so far I never did.

I come out by Exmouth Market and go past Sadler's Wells and through the Angel and come up to a junction and pass the Jamie Oliver restaurant. I see people relaxing there too but I'm on my way to work. All my life I have been on my way to work and seen people relaxing and having coffee and I don't stop.

I'm going up up up up up and that's the way it is all the way and then I come to the brow of the hill of Liverpool Road and then it's downhill all the way – and there always seem to be police cars going down there with the siren blaring on a call. And then I come to Holloway Road. I do a left and I'm at London Metropolitan University, where I work.

I cycle because it's cheaper. A Tube pass these days is very expensive. And because it clears my head. If I'm teaching I like to get on my bike. I can plan my day around my bike – I know when I'm going to arrive. It cuts out walking to the Tube. It cuts out crowds. You're in your own mental space as a cyclist. It invigorates. I don't think about getting fit or anything like that but cycling wakes you up in the morning – it's your horse – and in the evening it winds you down.

Stories London commuters tell themselves
(as they look through the train/bus/tram window)

1. I live in a world-class metropolis; this is the price I pay for that immense privilege.
2. I am green. I am good. I am not in a car.
3. This is actually quite fast.
4. Saturday.
5. TV tonight.
6. Look at all these people around me – they're all the same, they're all unlike me.
7. Lunch.
8. This is for money and money means happiness.
9. I belong to the established moral order; to conform is to be good.
10. Friday.
11. One day I'll just turn around, not get on, and run away, and be free.
12. Thursday.
13. A working-class hero is something to be.
14. Imagine what commuting is like in the Third World.
15. Dinner.

The drivers

21,000 licensed 'black cabs' operating in London and 25,000 licensed cab drivers. 50,000 mini cab drivers.

20,000 bus drivers driving 7,500 buses on more than 700 routes.

Tube drivers: 3,193 train operators, 85 trainee train operators, and 3,278 overall.

The inside of an omnibus

There are also certain things which almost all omnibus passengers do; such as help ladies to and fro; gradually get nearer to the door whenever a vacant seat occurs, so as to force the new comer further up than he likes; and all people stumble, forward or sideways, when they first come in, and the coach sets off before they are seated. Among the pleasures, are seeing the highly satisfied faces of persons suddenly relieved from a long walk; being able to read a book; and, occasionally, observing one of a congenial sort in the hands of a fellow-passenger. Among the evils, are dirty boots and wetting umhrellas; broken panes of glass in bad weather, afflicting the napes of the necks of invalids; and fellows who endeavour to convenience themselves at everybody's expense, by taking up as much room as possible, and who pretend to alter their oblique position when remonstrated with, without really doing it. Item, cramps in the leg, when thrusting it excessively backwards underneath the seat, in making way for a new comer, – the patient thrusting it forth again with an agonized vivacity, that sets the man opposite him laughing.

Item, cruel treadings upon corns, the whole being of the old lady or gentleman seeming to be mashed into the burning foot, and the sufferer looking in an ecstasy of tormented doubt whether to be decently quiet or murderously vociferous, – the inflictor, meanwhile, thinking it sufficient to say, "Very sorry," in an indifferent tone of voice, and taking his seat with an air of luxurious complacency. Among the pleasures also, particularly in going home at night, must not be forgotten the having the omnibus finally to yourself, re-adjusting yourself in a corner betwixt slumbering and waking, and throwing up your feet on the seat opposite; though, as the will becomes piqued in proportion to its luxuries, you always regret that the seats are not wider, and that you cannot treat your hat, on cold nights, as freely as if it were a nightcap.

From Men, Women, and Books *(1847)*
by Leigh Hunt

Tube trivia

1. First train of the day into London: 4:53 from Upminster to Richmond, District line

2. Size of network: 249 miles, 402 kilometres

3. Number of stations: 270 (60 on the District, the most on any one line)

4. 45 per cent of the network is underground (either though cut and cover or in deep tunnels)

5. Deepest section of line: Holly Bush Hill, Hampstead, Northern line – 68.8 metres/221 feet

6. Longest elevator: Angel: 60m/197 feet, with a vertical rise of 27.5 metres/90 feet

7. Busiest junction: District and Circle triangle between South Kensington, Notting Hill Gate and Earl's Court.

8. Busiest Tube station: Waterloo, with 57,000 people passing through at the morning peak period, or 82 million people per year.

9. Number of trains operating at peak commuter times: 525 (morning); 527 (evening)

10. Number of people on network at any one time: 600,000 (more than the population of Oslo)

11. Newest line: Victoria line

12. Newest section: Jubilee line from Green Park to Stratford (1993–9)

13. Average speed: 20.5mph/33km per hour

14. Maximum speed: 60mph-plus on the Metropolitan Line

15. Total number of passengers carried each year: 1.1 billion

16. Trains timetabled 110 weeks in advance

17. Shortest distance between stops: 0.161 miles/0.3km Covent Garden to Leicester Square, Piccadilly line

18. Longest distance between stops: 3.9 miles/6.3km Chesham to Chalfont & Latimer, Metropolitan line

19. Temperatures recorded during the 2006 heatwave; 47°C/116°F (maximum temperature for transporting livestock: 35°C)

20. Last train at night out of London: 00:56 Earls Court to Ealing Broadway, District line

I'm not a number: today's trends

- In the UK, 67% of all commuting trips are made by car, 11% on foot, 9% by bus, 5% by surface rail and 4% by bicycle.
- In London, 37% of commuters travel by car, 19% by light rail/Underground, 15% by bus/coach, 14% by surface rail, 9% by foot and 4% by bicycle.
- The average UK journey time to work: 28 minutes.
- The average journey time to work for London residents: 41 minutes.
- On average, commuting trips on foot take 18 minutes, by bike 22 minutes, by car 24 minutes, by bus 41 minutes, and by surface rail 69 minutes.
- The average UK commuter spends 1266 miles/year doing it. In other words – in a lifetime: 41 minutes x twice a day x 5 days a week x 48 weeks a year x 44 years (age 21–65) = 1,731,840 minutes or 28,864 hours or 1202.66 days or three years and then some, on average!

Source: National Travel Survey – Department of Transport (2011)

The Postmodern passenger
(after Ihab Hassan)

Modern	Postmodern
Flâneur	Commuter
Zone 1	Suburb
Newspaper	Freesheet
Umbrella	Headphones
Signified	Signifer
Phallic	Androgynous
Seriousness	Banality
Metaphysics	Irony
Transcendence	Immanence
Purpose	Play
Elite	Everyman
Logos	Exhaustion/silence
Arrival	Journey
Car	Train
God	Spirit
Binary	Multiple
Adversarial	Communitarian
Terminus	Station

Timeline V

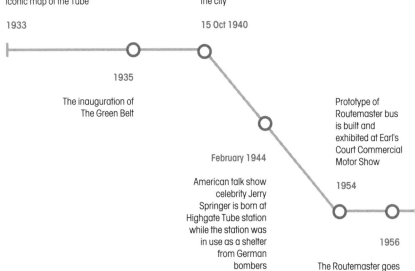

Harry Beck designs his
iconic map of the Tube

1933

Sixty-five shelterers
are killed in Balham
Tube station from a
direct bomb hit; three
months later 100
more are killed from a
direct hit at Bank
Station in the heart of
the city

15 Oct 1940

1935

The inauguration of
The Green Belt

February 1944

American talk show
celebrity Jerry
Springer is born at
Highgate Tube station
while the station was
in use as a shelter
from German
bombers

Prototype of
Routemaster bus
is built and
exhibited at Earl's
Court Commercial
Motor Show

1954

1956

The Routemaster goes
into passenger service

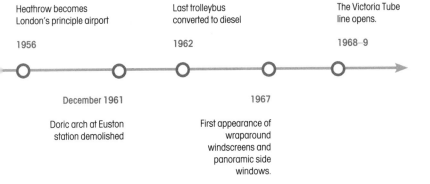

Heathrow becomes
London's principle airport

1956

Last trolleybus
converted to diesel

1962

The Victoria Tube
line opens.

1968–9

December 1961

Doric arch at Euston
station demolished

1967

First appearance of
wraparound
windscreens and
panoramic side
windows.

6

WORK

In every cry of every Man,

In every Infant's cry of fear,

In every voice, in every ban,

The mind-forg'd manacles I hear

From "London" (1794) by William Blake

During the last phase of the morning commute, the transformation is just about complete. As he emerges from the burrows of Bank, sweats his way across Oxford Circus, strolls across the Jubilee Bridge or hikes through Bloomsbury, the commuter sloughs off his travelling skin and assumes his working posture. The bed-wetter becomes a broker, the dreamer becomes a recruitment solutions provider, the lifelong singleton becomes a PR flirt, the dominatrix becomes a civil servant. We harden our hearts and we prepare: John Wemmick refuses to mention his castle when he is at work in *Great Expectations*, Verloc morphs from purveyor of pornography to political plotter as he walks to the embassy in Conrad's *The Secret Agent*.

For the commuter, work is London and London is work. On Saturday the capital can be retail or theatre, on Sunday it may be a museum. But Monday to Friday, between 7 or 8 or 9 or 10 and 4 or 5 or 6 or whatever, the city in the day is the job in hand. The London of work is not like the other Londons. In residential areas the boroughs are mapped out nodally. When the commuter and outlying Tube stations were built, concentrations of shops, pubs and services sprang up around them. They are still there. Beyond the clusters of services are streets packed with houses, thousands upon thousands of them, streets that look like linear car parks, others that ape the countryside, or warzones, or esplanades and post-industrial edgelands, which don't look like streets at all. Breaking up the terraced canyons, splashes of parkland, arches of trees, play areas and schools.

The work zone is vertical and concrete, anti-residential and adult. Its hubs – while sprouting from Tube and train stations and bus stops – are of an altogether different character, with specialisms spread around W1, SW1, WC2, the ECs. Money and insurance in the City; media and public relations in Fitzrovia and Soho; Silicon Roundabout at Old Street; IT incubators at Clerkenwell and

"Everyman is not Bunyan's Christian, Leopold Bloom, Winston Smith; Everyman is a commuter"

Shoreditch; Temple for the Law; Belgravia's diplomats, Victoria Street's civil servants. Retail opportunities are carpet bombed all over town. Some 1.4 million people live in the centre, and around two million people travel in to Zone 1 every day for work. Another 2.8 million people are on the move to jobs in other parts of London. Just under 7,400 live in the City of London and the daytime population is around 350,000. Everyman is not Bunyan's Christian, Leopold Bloom, Winston Smith; Everyman is a commuter.

London is a multifarious city. Its people are inscrutable. The cliché of the besuited commuter on his way to the City fits the period 6:30–8am perhaps, but once that stage is over there follow the clerical staff, lawyers, computer programmers, designers and journalists, then chefs, actors, musicians. And before any of these come the coffee makers and croissant heaters, preparing fuel and sustenance. There is also the ghost commute: those who go off in the opposite direction, on buses to pick spuds in Surrey fields, pilots and stewardesses on the first Tube to Heathrow, the drivers themselves, bound for Upminster, Morden, Ruislip and the bus garages.

The workers' train is long-gone, but classes persist, as workers are stratifed by hours, clothes, pay and conditions. Overland trains have retained their first-class coaches, and bus routes are like studies in class structure: ethnicities, occupations, destinies alter and commingle as a bus passes through London's boroughs. The Tube train is the great leveller. We meet up in the morning at the terminal stations and everything merges. Then we get off and regroup in our hierarchies.

More than 2.5 million people do, though, work in offices. In *Something Happened* (1974), Joseph Heller penned a notorious set-piece about office politics that runs: "In the office in which I work there are five people of whom I am afraid. Each of these five people is afraid of four people (excluding overlaps), for a total of twenty, and each of these twenty people is afraid of six people, making a total of one hundred and twenty people who are feared by at least one person. Each of these one hundred and twenty people is afraid of the other one hundred and nineteen, and all of these one hundred and forty-five people are afraid of the twelve men at the top who helped found and build the company and now own and direct it."

Fear, in a world of specious hierarchies, takeovers, redundancies and recessions, is human; even a small group of people compelled to co-habit in a limited space will generate tensions, tyrannies, deceit and conniving. But in surveys, most Londoners like, or say they like, their jobs (unsurprising given the constant reminders in the media that their city is the only place enjoying prosperity in the whole of the UK). The success of the 2001–3 television series *The Office* was partly due to people laughing at themselves, but it was equally a smug recognition that most offices are not quite as bad as the one overseen by David Brent. His cod-Dostoevsky definition of the workplace – "Put the key of despair into the lock of apathy. Turn the knob of mediocrity slowly and open the gates of despondency – welcome to a day in the average office" – wouldn't be in the least bit funny if it were believed to be true. Office-dwellers are either deeply satisfied, or so deeply deluded that it doesn't matter.

But there's a lot to be said for offices. Most come with hot coffee and cool drinking water, free central heating, a

social life, sexual frissons, a computer, a free phone-line, a desk, a chair, maybe a view – and you get praised for attending regularly and punctually, like school. You also get paid. Work – the specific daily activity – varies, but office chit-chat is universal. Bosses, money, holidays, relationships, vices, virtues, lunch, drinks – and, of course, the commute, are the staple – but rich – themes riffed on in the kitchens and around the water fountains every morning and evening.

Before I finally gave up on working in offices during my first stint in London, in the late 1980s, I tried the Civil Service, joining the Ministry of Defence at Empress State Building in Earl's Court as an EO, or Executive Officer. The job title was, like all job titles in government, ironic. There I met a man who commuted every day from Doncaster. He was, to me, a tragicomic hero. "It's home," he said. "I wouldn't want to move my family to London." He said he ate a cooked breakfast on the train and then got some extra sleep. At night he barely had time for dinner before going to bed. He lived his life upside down and back to front. The journey, now, from Doncaster station to King's Cross takes 2 hours and 57 minutes. Add on an hour perhaps for the extra trips from/to home and on the Tube from/to Earl's Court. The current season ticket price is £11,520. I don't know what the hero earned but he didn't look very senior to me.

Did he give up and go home? Or bring his family to Ealing or Clapham? I never found out. I left shortly after meeting him, having completed only six months of service ∎

The money

Average salaries. Sources: Reed; House of Commons; Goodman Masson; Telegraph

Barrister £500,000

Governer of the Bank of England £480,000

Pilot (captain) £100,000

General Practitioner £95,000

Banker £58,747–£870,000 plus bonuses

MP £66,396 plus expenses

Tube train driver £42,424

Publisher £37,793

Nurse £28,334

Schoolteacher £27,000

Journalist £26,077

Fitness instructor £21,000

Barista £17,038

Thirty Bob a Week

For like a mole I journey in the dark,
A-travelling along the underground
From my Pillar'd Halls and broad Suburban Park,
To come the daily dull official round;
And home again at night with my pipe all alight,
A-scheming how to count ten bob a pound.

John Davidson (1894)

Working class ticket please!

The first train services were too expensive for working men. Things began to change, slowly and gradually, from 1838, when third-class travel became an option. The Railway Regulation Act of 1844 forced train companies to provide a roof on these carriages. From 1864 on, a series of Acts of Parliament obliged companies opening new railway lines to provide convenient and cheap trains for London's artisans, mechanics and labourers of both sexes.

The Great Northern carried clerks from Hornsey, Finchley, Southgate and Wood Green into King's Cross, which had opened 1852. Third-class return tickets cost 4d to 8d. The Great Eastern, in contrast, had to build a new station, Liverpool Street at Bishopsgate – opened in 1874 – and return fares on its morning services from Edmonton, Forest Gate, Ilford, Stanford Hill, Tottenham and Walthamstow started at 2d. The cheap trains drew working-class families and changed the look of the neighbourhoods. New housing schemes like Noel Park near Wood Green were established to provide tenements for the burgeoning new suburbanites. By 1884, the Great Eastern was carrying more than a quarter of London's working-class commuters.

On the underground, a similar pattern evolved. In May 1864, the Metropolitan Railway provided two workmen's trains, at 5:30am and 5:40am, operating from Paddington. The managers soon realised that there was good money to be made. Though the Cheap Trains Act of 1884 obliged the company to run two workmen's trains, it opted to run twelve. The same law obliged the Metropolitan District to operate one; it ran five. The plan paid off. Between 1882 and 1899, the number of workmen's tickets issued on the Metropolitan Railway jumped from 1,416,500 to more than 7,360,000. On the Metropolitan District the figure leapt from just over 630,000 to over 3,200,000. On London's first Tube, the City & South London, 500,000 workers travelled on special tickets in 1893. Six years later, 1,600,000 used the service.

As Simon Abernethy points out in his paper *Class and Commuting on the Underground, 1863–1939*, "The Underground arranged its fares to promote suburban development, with relatively higher fares for short distance travel in the centre than long distance travel to the suburbs." Thus, the suburban lines effected a sort of social control when it came to building and the distribution of the population. Class prejudices about where the poor should live survived well into the twentieth century. In 1938 Frank Pick, vice-chairman of the recently created London Passenger Transport Board, was questioned by a Royal Commission as to why the Underground did not offer a flat rate fare, as was the practice in New York. Pick objected that the New York Subway had "put what are relatively slums down in the Bronx instead of houses". He described these as "a kind of development there which is not too good".

Not everyone was pleased with the democratisation of transport in London. Clerics, MPs and first-class passengers objected to the fact that working class men and women were forced to travel at close quarters in the same carriage and also to the use of first and second class carriages as a default back-up system: workers sometimes strayed into the smarter carriages, which the law permitted on busy services.

But their complaints were short-lived. Workers' and cheap trains were on their way out. The Midland Railway abolished second-class travel in 1875, upgrading third-class passengers to second-class standards. Other companies followed its example. Second-class disappeared from fare tables until 1956, when third-class was renamed second. British Rail later renamed this standard class.

Beggars leaving town for their workhouse.

The Workhouse Clock: An Allegory

There's a murmur in the air,
And noise in every street –
The murmur of many tongues,
The noise of numerous feet –
While round the Workhouse door
The Labouring Classes flock,
For why? The Overseer of the Poor
Is setting the Workhouse Clock.

Who does not hear the tramp
Of thousands speeding along

Of either sex and various stamp,
Sickly, cripple, or strong,
Walking, limping, creeping
From court and alley, and lane,
But all in one direction sweeping
Like rivers that seek the main?

Who does not see them sally
From mill, and garret, and room,
In lane, and court and alley,
From homes in poverty's lowest valley,
Furnished with shuttle and loom –
Poor slaves of Civilisation's galley –
And in the road and footways rally,
As if for the Day of Doom?
Some, of hardly human form,
Stunted, crooked, and crippled by toil;
Dingy with smoke and dust and oil,
And smirch'd besides with vicious soil,
Clustering, mustering, all in a swarm.

…Onward, onward, with hasty feet,
They swarm – and westward still –
Masses born to drink and eat,
But starving amidst Whitechapel's meat,
And famishing down Cornhill!
Through the Poultry – but still unfed –
Christian Charity, hang your head!
Hungry – passing the Street of Bread;
Thirsty – the street of Milk;
Ragged – beside the Ludgate Mart,
So gorgeous, through Mechanic-Art,
With cotton, and wool, and silk!

Extract (1844) by Thomas Hood

Sandwiched

There are as many causes for the insidious and unstoppable rise of the sandwich as there are fillings. Londoners have eaten triangles and squares of bread, butter and meat, fish, cheese and suchlike on the go since Victorian times, when the trade of vending sandwiches appealed to those who wanted to work independently but had limited investments available. "The capital required to start in the trade was small," writes Mayhew. "A few pounds of ham, a proportion of loaves, and a little mustard was all that was required, and for this 10s was ample."

The ease of production and speedy delivery also suits a city that has always moved at a frantic pace and where food producers need a healthy turnover to pay high rents.

George Augustus Sala, in *Gaslight and Daylight* (1859), writes of the "amusement and instruction I derive from watching the performances in the ham and beef shop at the corner of Bow Street. Here are crowds of customers, hot and hungry from the Lyceum or Drury Lane, and clamorous for sandwiches. Ham sandwiches, beef sandwiches, German sausage sandwiches – legions of sandwiches are cut and consumed. The cry is 'mustard', anon the coppers rattle, and payment is tendered and change given." The British Sandwich Association (BSA) says that caffeine-fuelled city workers today won't wait longer than two minutes for their snatched lunches.

The originator of the British version, John Montagu, 4th Earl of Sandwich (1718–92), is said to have requested a meal of beef and bread that wouldn't interfere with his gambling. In reality the bread-wrapped meal comes to us from the Middle East via the eastern Mediterranean. Like the empanada and the pasty, the corner of the sandwich can be held between the fingers to keep the food clean. Only now, modern sandwich-eaters tend to swallow the dirty bits too.

The BSA claims that in one year 3,250,000,000 sandwiches are purchased from retail or catering outlets to the value of over £6,500,000,000 and that around a fifth of these are sold in London. The first "packaged" sandwich is believed to have been launched by Marks & Spencer in 1985 and the biggest current retailer is Subway. Trends suggest ham and egg are gaining on chicken in the filling stakes.

There could be psychological reasons underpinning the success of the lunchtime sandwich. There is little guilt in a small, quickly-consumed snack. It's a way of proving to your boss/spouse/self/colleagues that you're at work to work, not to dine or, God forbid, enjoy a drink. Perhaps, too, the tri-level concoction is a mirror of other features of the city worker's life. After all, is not work a layer of filling between two slender commutes? And is not life itself a choice but soon-extinguished snack enjoyed between two slices of the eternal?

Most popular sandwich fillings

in the pre-prepared market

Chicken (24%)
Fish (18%)
Cheese (15%)
Ham (12%)
Bacon (10%)
Egg (7%)
Sausage (3%)

Source: British Sandwich Association

He that tilleth his land shall be satisfied with bread: but he that followeth vain persons is void of understanding

Proverbs 12:11

Eight hours

"Eight hours work, eight hours sleep, eight hours play, make a just and healthy day."

Attributed to the ninth-century king Alfred the Great

"Eight hours labour, eight hours recreation, eight hours rest."

*Said to have been the motto of the nineteenth-century
social reformer Robert Owen*

"Eight hours for work, eight hours for education and leisure, eight hours for sleep, what a reasonable programme!"

Chinese Communist propaganda leaflet of 1924

A skinny decaf soya life

The coffee chains are not really cafés in the romantic sense of the word. They have no heritage, no quiet corners, are short on décor as well as decorum, and the customers are the only people employed, unpaid, as waiters. And they don't really sell coffee at all.

Every morning the commuter must, like a goldfish, try to forget that he's on the same journey on the same line to the same job. This act of faith is powerfully religious, almost kenotic in its self-abnegation. A similar wilfulness lies behind his decision to stand in line at a designated point between commute and workplace – Costa, Pret, Nero, Italia, Starbucks, Monmouth, the independent outlet…he has his favourite – to collect his bucket of scorched milk. He accepts the programmed welcome from the continental cashier – who, he can't help thinking, might know a thing or two about cafés, ristrettos, garçons and also tips – asks for his drink – a latte, please, that's "lah-tay" with a long "aaaahhhh", pays ten times the cost of production, and shuffles along to collect the hot Styrofoam container (half-life: 100 years).

The flavour does vary – sometimes it is like Horlicks, sometimes it has a hint of arsenic, sometimes it is sweet even before the tubes of sugar are decanted – but it is always, reliably, absolutely awful. Disappointment is assured. This is how the Londoner has appropriated the continental breakfast – he has made it hot, fast, flavourless, anti-social, uncomfortable, expensive, and with at least one queue every time he goes for a refill. And yet, there is a bizarre confidence in the capital's café culture. There's something of the chicken tikka about the whole operation, and not only because that's another possible accidental flavour when you experiment thermodynamically with semi-skimmed. It's all there in that latte, or cortado, or flat white, or syrupy soya-laced confection. London absorbs all cultures, all traditions, all flavours and repackages them as creamy white blandness.

The Coffee Shop
Punch (19th August 1882)

Q. What is a Coffee-Shop?

A. The opprobrium of the London thoroughfares.

Q. May I ask you to particularise a little?

A. It is difficult in a few words to define so curious a combination of many nastinesses as the London Coffee-Shop. It can only be described, and that in considerable detail.

Q. Is it not, as its name implies, a shop for the sale of Coffee?

A. That would, in most cases, be an imperfect and misleading definition. Firstly, because most Coffee-Shops sell other things than Coffee. Secondly, and most importantly, because most Coffee-Shops do not sell Coffee at all.

Q. But does not this singular carrying out of the *lucus a non lucendo* principle lead to difficulties with would-be customers?

A. Not at all.

Q. How, then, do the keepers of Coffee-Houses avoid such difficulties?

A. By substituting various dirty and dismal decoctions which they vend under the name of the genuine produce of Mocha.

Charles Dickens joins the rush hour

…the early clerk population of Somers and Camden Towns, Islington and Pentonville, are fast pouring into the city… Middle aged men, whose salaries have by no means increased in the same proportion as their families, plod steadily along, apparently with no object in view but the counting house…

From Sketches by Boz *(1836)*

The Hours

When do Londoners start work?

Smithfields meat trader: **9pm**

Baker: **10pm**

Tube train driver: **5am**

Stockbroker: **7am**

Barista: **7am**

Banker: **8am**

Builder: **8am**

Schoolteacher: **8:30am**

Shop assistant: **8:30am**

Bank manager: **9am**

Civil servant: **9am**

Head chef: **9am**

MP and IT, PR and media professional: **10am**

Newspaper reporter, editor: **noon**

Olive Schreiner on equal opportunities

The primitive male might discuss with her his success in hunting and her success in finding roots; as the primitive peasant may discuss today with his wife the crops and cows in which both are equally interested and which both understand; there is nothing in their order of life to produce always increasingly divergent habits of thought and interest.

In modern civilised life, in many sections, the lack of any common labour and interests and the wide dissimilarity of the life led by the man and the woman, tend continually to produce increasing divergence; so that, long before middle life is reached, they are left without any bond of co-cohesion but that of habit. The comradeship and continual stimulation, rising from intercourse with those sharing our closest interests and regarding life from the same standpoint, the man tends to seek in his club and among his male companions, and the woman accepts solitude, or seeks dissipations which tend yet farther to disrupt the common conjugal life. A certain mental *camaraderie* and community of impersonal interests is imperative in conjugal life in addition to a purely sexual relation, if the union is to remain a living and always growing reality. It is more especially because the sharing by woman of the labours of man will tend to promote *camaraderie* and the existence of common, impersonal interests and like habits of thought and life, that the entrance of women into the very fields shared by men, and not into others peculiarly reserved for her, is so desirable.

From Women and Labour *(1911)*

The Drain and Bank Complex

It might sound like the kind of psychological disease a City commuter risks ending his career with, but the Drain – or Waterloo and City line – and Bank Complex (Bank and Monument stations and their assorted lines) function together to form one of the capital's key mass transit conduits for populating the Square Mile. The Central Line, Northern (City Branch), Waterloo and City line and Docklands Light Railway all converge at Bank, as do at least 19 bus routes. Monument, only 400 yards away, is on the District and Circle lines.

By 1876 the two existing underground railways – the Metropolitan and Metropolitan District – had reached Aldgate and Mansion House, respectively. These inner-London lines connecting several rail termini were known as the "Inner Circle". The station at Monument opened with the name Eastcheap on 6th October 1884 but was renamed Monument on 1st November.

The backers who had financed these schemes wanted a line to the heart of the City. In 1898, the Waterloo & City Railway opened a new station, with platforms under Queen Victoria Street, originally called City. The line became known as the Drain because, as London's second deep-level Tube, it was a novelty for those working along it, or perhaps due to water dripping into the tunnel from the Thames above. The City and South London Railway (the precursor of the Northern Line) opened its own station, called Bank, on 25th January 1900. The subterranean works meant the builders had to remove human remains from the crypt of St Mary Woolnoth church to make space for a ticket hall and lift shafts. On 30th July of the same year, the Central London Railway opened its new terminus at Bank. The proximity of the Bank of England, Royal Exchange and Mansion House precluded any surface works and the sub-surface operations were very costly for all concerned. One of the consequences was the lack of a lift up to the exit, resulting in a sloping floor from the Waterloo and City platforms that proved unpopular with passengers.

To avoid claims from building owners above, the platforms beneath Threadneedle Street and Poultry curve sharply. The southern end of the City and South London Railway platforms was close to Monument station and on 18th September 1933, a connecting escalator link was built. In 1960, Bank was the first place in Europe to have a Trav-o-lator – a moving walkway, patented by the lift company Otis – installed on its sloping corridor. In 1991, the DLR connection opened at Bank.

Some 96,000 people move through Bank and Monument every morning – 40,000 of them changing trains – making it the fourth busiest interchange on the Tube. Close by are Cannon Street and Fenchurch Street. City Thameslink, Liverpool Street, London Bridge and Moorgate stations are within walking distance.

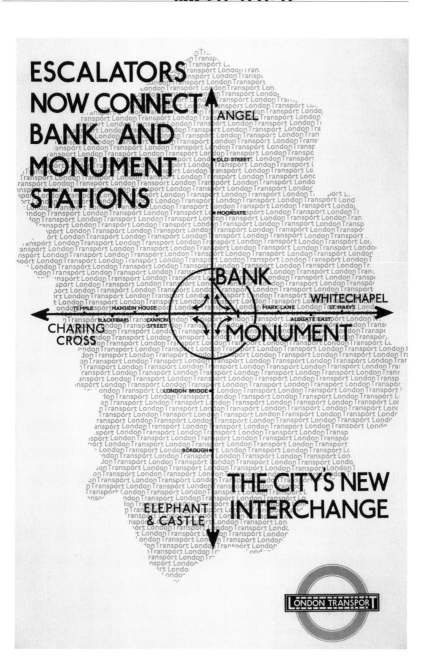

ESCALATORS NOW CONNECT BANK AND MONUMENT STATIONS

BANK

MONUMENT

THE CITY'S NEW INTERCHANGE

LONDON TRANSPORT

Greater London's road bridges

Upriver, down the centuries

London c. 50 AD (rebuilt 12th, 19th and 20th centuries)
Kingston 12th century, possibly earlier (rebuilt 1828)
Putney 1729 (rebuilt 1886)
Westminster 1750 (rebuilt 1862)
Blackfriars 1769 (rebuilt 1869)
Richmond 1777
Hammersmith 1827 (rebuilt 1887)
Albert 1873
Wandsworth 1873 (rebuilt 1940)
Tower 1894
Vauxhall 1906
Southwark 1921
Lambeth 1932
Chiswick 1933
Hampton Court 1933
Twickenham 1933
Chelsea 1937
Waterloo 1945
Queen Elizabeth II (Dartford Crossing) 1991

Work and Modes through the ages

ERA	JOB	THE COMMUTE
Pre-Roman	Hunter-gatherer (him) Fire-kindler (her)	Soles of feet
Roman AD 43–410 (Londinium)	Olive oil trader (him) Prostitute (her)	Sandals, ox-cart
Anglo-Saxon 410–1066 (Lundenwic/Lundenburh)	Potter (him) Cup-bearer (her)	Donkey
Medieval 1066–1485	Fletcher (him) Nun (her)	Packhorse, Palfrey
Tudor & Stuart 1485–1714	Lawyer (him) Washerwoman (her)	Sedan chair, coach and horses, wherry, barge
Eighteenth century	Clockmaker (him) Midwife (her)	Short-stage coach
Nineteenth century (Victorian)	Copper (him) Novelist (her)	Horse-drawn omnibus, cut-and-cover underground steam train, horse-drawn and cable tram
Early twentieth century	Chartered accountant (him) Secretary (her)	Diesel train, electric commuter train, electric tram, deep-level tube, taxi, bus
Late twentieth century (Thatcher and Blair)	Broker (him) Barrister (her)	Car, railway, aeroplane, helicopter, motorbike, minibus, inline skates, SUV
Twenty-first century	Blogger (him) Barista (her)	Hybrid bicycle, scooter, Segway

THE CITY GENT: STRIPPED

6. CUFFLINKS

Cufflinks may appear discreet and inoffensive but when you see them you know you are in the presence of a Nietzschean SuperGent. Proof of a willingness to pay attention to detail very early in the morning, they claim on behalf of their wearer a self-absorbed calm: I breakfasted, I listened to talk radio, I had time to don my cufflinks ergo I belong to another era/universe. When, in the eighteenth centuy, the shirt evolved from its status as an undergarment to being displayed, it was considered frivolously bad form to reveal the sleeves. Cuff buttons often contained painted miniatures, including portraits of loved ones or well-known figures, and they could be hidden away. The modern cufflink reflects back the smiling confidence of the wearer – the true loved one – for whom the dainty manacles bestow an ironic freedom. While the vast majority of people buy or unearth their ancestral cufflinks for weddings, balls or special occasions, the daily wearer knows that work, life,

even commuting, are in themselves galas and perfomances worthy of ornamentation. Part of the standard uniform of bankers, lawyers and directors, they are used by young studs to exhibit their deep yearning to belong to the higher castes. There is something quasi-Masonic about the glint of a cufflink, the wearer seeming to say, "This is the club I belong to, I make no concessions to practicality. You wouldn't catch me dead in buttons." Stiffness as stylishness, fussiness as fashion statement, smallness as heft: two little metallic dumb-bells piercing the great flaps of Frenchified Jermyn Street fabric around the wrist send out a signal as resonant as any probation-server's ankle tether.

Train tweet

Jonni @jonnilondon

Obviously didn't realise I'd put on my invisible coat this morning.
GET OUT OF MY WAY!!
#London #commute #slowpeople

Friedrich Engels visits London

A town, such as London, where a man may wander for hours together without reaching the beginning of the end, without meeting the slightest hint which could lead to the inference that there is open country within reach, is a strange thing.

This colossal centralisation, this heaping together of two and a half millions of human beings at one point, has multiplied the power of this two and a half millions a hundredfold; has raised London to the commercial capital of the world, created the giant docks and assembled the thousand vessels that continually cover the Thames. I know nothing more imposing than the view which the Thames offers during the ascent from the sea to London Bridge. The masses of buildings, the wharves on both sides, especially from Woolwich upwards, the countless ships along both shores, crowding ever closer and closer together, until, at last, only a narrow passage remains in the middle of the river, a passage through which hundreds of steamers shoot by one another; all this is so vast, so impressive, that a man cannot collect himself, but is lost in the marvel of England's greatness before he sets foot upon English soil.

The hundreds of thousands of all classes and ranks crowding past each other, are they not all human beings with the same qualities and powers, and with the same interest in being happy? And have they not, in the end, to seek happiness in the same way, by the same means? And still they crowd by one another as though they had nothing in common, nothing to do with one another, and their only agreement is the tacit one, that each keep to his own side of the pavement, so as not to delay the opposing streams of the crowd, while it occurs to no man to honour another with so much as a glance… The dissolution of mankind into monads, of which each one has a separate principle, the world of atoms, is here carried out to its utmost extreme.

From The Condition of the Working Class in England *(1845), trans. Florence Kelley Wischnewetzky*

Timeline VI

TV series *Metro-land*,
written and narrated by
poet laureate John
Betjeman, screens

26 February 1973

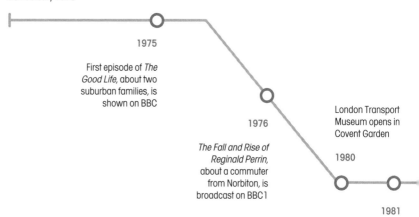

1975

First episode of *The
Good Life*, about two
suburban families, is
shown on BBC

1976

*The Fall and Rise of
Reginald Perrin*,
about a commuter
from Norbiton, is
broadcast on BBC1

London Transport
Museum opens in
Covent Garden

1980

1981

Zonal fares
introduced by Greater
London Council
leader Ken
Livingstone

Introduction of the
Travelcard season
ticket

1983

Introduction of the
one day Travelcard

1984

1984

One-person operation
is phased in on Tube
stations meaning
there are fewer
conductors and the
train driver becomes
responsible for the
doors

July 1984

Smoking banned on
trains; this is soon
extended to platforms
and finally to entire
stations

7

OUT

Soames used the Underground again

in going home. The fog was worse than ever

at Sloane Square station...

"Will u b home for T-time?"
"I'll get a takeaway don't wait up"

The journey home is Pavlovian, the commuter licking his lips at the anticipation of food and wine, television and bed. Every evening he feels he is someone "who has been long in city pent". Having performed a multitude of roles – servant, trader, victim, bawler, brawler, engineer, executive, clown, tyrant – he is ready to slip into a near-Caliban state. If being at work is about occupying the "esteem" level in Maslow's hierarchy of needs, home is a purely physiological space: he wants now to consume, excrete, sleep, and perhaps love and make love.

But first he has to get there. Where the morning rush is controlled and narrowly themed around getting to work, with each commuter following his or her private trails, the early-evening peak hour is chaotic and collective. In the centre there are a few dozen Tube stations, a sprinkling of car parks, 18 overland rail termini. Everybody seems to be heading for the same place at the same time. The city metamorphoses for the great Exodus. Entrances to stations look like storm drains or siphons, taxis become beautiful, buses come in fives.

Branches of Marks & Spencer Simply Food have re-stocked their shelves, crayfish salads and hoi-sin wraps targeted as carefully as a sniper's rifle. Everything is structured to provide an easy-flow gauntlet of selection, speed queuing and spending. The Waterloo Station branch has one of the highest footfalls per square metre in the country. For tired parents, skint nurses, teachers armed with sheafs of marking to complete, food can become the most an evening can offer. Mobile phone calls and texts are curt: "Will you get a pizza?" "Have got the rocket." "Will u b home for T-time?" "I'll get a take away don't wait up."

At the other end of the journey, the liquor merchants prepare. Oddbins used to own half of Surbiton station. Sometimes they'd open a side door – which probably once led to a waiting room or a bathroom – and you'd be surrounded by wines, barrels bearing offers, a parquet floor to suggest a vague French provincial touch. Alcohol is the chief lubricant

that ensures the continuing operation of the commuter system.

It's not always smoothly from London. When something goes wrong at Waterloo Station, the commute – that fluid and linear structure – quickly falls apart. A solitary train breakdown, a body on the line or a copper-collecting thief can stop all movement, turning the concourse into a simmering riot of anger and despair, and the parked carriag-

es into a railway version of Julio Cortázar's famous story about a never-ending traffic jam on the *autoroute* into Paris.

Somehow, though, millions of souls escape. The leaving trains have their own moods: excitement, apprehension and a sense of liberation mix with fatigue and hunger. But there has to be a kernel of deep optimism at the bottom of it all. This, after all, this journey home is what it's all for... ■

THE CITY GENT: STRIPPED

7. THE SHIRT

The twin dart, double plackets and split yokes of Jermyn Street tailoring-as-tyranny are almost extinct but the shirt is the great survivor. Suits are outgrown or saved for special occasions, ties are loosened or cast aside, and the hats and the brollies of the old-world city worker are rarely seen. But the shirt collar remains. It is the common denominator of a bureaucratic vocation, the foundation and canvas. White and newly pressed it can stand as visible proof of seriousness and understated smartness. It can look Mormonish or hint at a schoolboy past: naughty but naïve. It can be scarily neutral or classic. Perhaps the white shirt's seeming ambiguity is the reason some gents choose to wear shirts with checked patterns in lurid colours along with a tie in a different hue and featuring wave-like swirls, all in order to create a geometric event on arrival at the office.

Two-tone (1970s) and fat-striped (1980s) shirts now hang in charity shops, mementoes of ex-hippies and ageing yuppies. Some will be bought by retro-minded students, wearing workwear for play. The shirt is itself role-playing with the wearer's torso. It began as an undergarment in the Middle Ages and only came to the fore in the eighteenth century. At first the sleeves were fluffy and loose, but they were tucked in, and collars were tightened, and soon the cambric blouse became the slim-fit, bri-nylon body-stocking. Notwithstanding, the shirt likes to declare its bawdy memories: in twenty-first century films women still don men's shirts after The First Night.

The shirt expresses a work ethic: the collar serves as a grime-recorder, evidence of pollution and graft. It denotes leisure too: the tails are allowed to escape and flap about on the later trains to indicate freedom and generosity of spirit, rebellion or debauchery. Collar sizes come and go: one decade it is long and dangling, the next it is trim and tidy. It can be buttoned down and immobile or can free itself and spread its gape, wantonly, all over the lapels of a jacket. Only the shirt-aesthete knows the names: Ascot, Cambridge, Henley, Middlesex, New Cranford, Newmarket, Rugby. White collars named for white-collar places.

Outside the boardroom, the Ainsley medium-spread collar dominates; not so otiose as to suggest reticence nor so strident as to catch in a fire door. In the 1990s, an attempt was made by some office workers in the arts to wear black shirts and, even, black pullovers, but a withering press campaign put an end to all that. Currently, directors in media firms in the West End like to wear floral shirts, but this, too, will be for only a limited time. Collar, cuff, pattern, detail, logo – all these are but the trappings of time passing. Plain colours, likewise, change with the whims of the seasons. A white shirt is like a white sheet of paper. The final word on everything. The shroud.

A rush hour

Monday evening, 5–6pm, Waterloo Station

WATERLOO STATION IS THE BUSIEST IN THE UK, WITH 94,045,510 ENTRIES AND EXITS IN 2011–2012.

17:00	PORTSMOUTH HARBOUR
17:01	LONDON WATERLOO VIA RICHMOND & KINGSTON (circular route)
17:02	GUILDFORD VIA WOKING
17:02	GUILDFORD VIA COBHAM
17:05	ALDERSHOT
17:05	POOLE & WEYMOUTH
17:06	HAMPTON COURT
17:07	LONDON WATERLOO VIA HOUNSLOW & RICHMOND (circular route)
17:09	EFFINGHAM JUNCTION VIA EPSOM
17:09	PORTSMOUTH HARBOUR VIA BASINGSTOKE
17:12	BASINGSTOKE
17:12	SHEPPERTON
17:13	LONDON WATERLOO VIA RICHMOND & KINGSTON (circular route)
17:15	FRATTON
17:15	LONDON WATERLOO VIA RICHMOND & HOUNSLOW (circular route)
17:16	CHESSINGTON SOUTH
17:20	EXETER ST DAVID'S
17:20	READING
17:20	WOKING
17:22	WEYBRIDGE VIA HOUNSLOW & STAINES
17:23	BASINGSTOKE
17:24	DORKING (MAIN)
17:25	ALTON
17:27	LONDON WATERLOO VIA KINGSTON & RICHMOND (circular route)
17:23	BASINGSTOKE
17:24	DORKING (MAIN)
17:25	ALTON
17:27	LONDON WATERLOO VIA KINGSTON & RICHMOND (circular route)
17:28	WINDSOR & ETON RIVERSIDE
17:30	EPSOM (SURREY)
17:30	PORTSMOUTH HARBOUR
17:31	LONDON WATERLOO VIA RICHMOND & KINGSTON (circular route)
17:32	GUILDFORD VIA WOKING

17:32	GUILDFORD VIA COBHAM
17:35	POOLE & WEYMOUTH
17:35	READING
17:36	HAMPTON COURT
17:37	LONDON WATERLOO VIA HOUNSLOW & RICHMOND (circular route)
17:39	EFFINGHAM JUNCTION VIA EPSOM
17:39	PORTSMOUTH HARBOUR VIA BASINGSTOKE
17:41	BASINGSTOKE
17:42	SHEPPERTON
17:43	SHEPPERTON VIA RICHMOND
17:45	HAVANT
17:45	LONDON WATERLOO VIA RICHMOND & HOUNSLOW (circular route)
17:46	CHESSINGTON SOUTH
17:48	SOUTHAMPTON CENTRAL
17:50	READING
17:50	WOKING
17:50	YEOVIL JUNCTION
17:52	WEYBRIDGE VIA HOUNSLOW & STAINES
17:53	BASINGSTOKE
17:54	DORKING (MAIN)
17:55	ALTON
17:57	LONDON WATERLOO VIA KINGSTON & RICHMOND (circular route)
17:58	WINDSOR & ETON RIVERSIDE
18:00	EPSOM (SURREY)
18:00	PORTSMOUTH HARBOUR

- London Victoria Station is the second busiest, with 76,231,290 entries and exits.
- The third busiest is London Liverpool Street, with 57,106,502 entries and exits.
- Gare du Nord station in France is Europe's busiest, with 190 million entries and exits.
- Shinjuku station in Tokyo tops 1.377 billion.
- At Clapham Junction 21,609,997 people change trains per year, making it the busiest station for interchanges. It is also the busiest station in Europe by track activity, with 2,000 trains per day, most of which make a stop: one train every 13 seconds passes or stops at peak times and one train passes or stops every 30 seconds at off-peak times.

Sources: Office of Rail Regulation; National Rail Enquiries; Le Figaro

Rush hour

Source: Transport for London

Peak
Monday–Friday 04:30–09:29

Off-peak
Monday–Friday 09:30–04:29 (the following day);
Saturdays, Sundays and public holidays
04:30–04:29 (the following day)

The cost of commuting

Source: Passenger Focus, Transport for London

Sample of annual pass prices – station-to-station;
Travelcard is extra; fastest times given.

Zone1–6 Travelcard £2,224
Surbiton–London Waterloo (17 mins) £1,708
Hove–London Victoria (1hr 4 mins) £3,280
Portsmouth–London Waterloo (1hr 42 mins) £4,668
Canterbury West–St Pancras International (56 mins) £4,904
Peterborough–London King's Cross (53 mins) £5,560
Kettering–St Pancras International (53 mins) £6,220
Swindon–London Paddington (56 mins) £7,760

And first class?
Swindon–London St Pancras £16,540
Wadhurst–London Terminals £6,584

Baker Street Station buffet

And all that day in murky London Wall
The thought of Ruislip kept him warm inside
John Betjeman (1954)

Flash-fiction

From "The London Clock", a collaborative challenge to create a literary day,
edited by Holly Clarke, www.londonlitproject.com

17:38 ON YOUR MARKS! SARAH MELLEMY (2012)

Unseemly elbowing amongst the cyclists sets the tone. Game on! I weave between double-deckers and jump lights, piston-legs pump homewards. "It's Friday, Friday…!" Terrible song urges me on. Ironic handle-bar streamers flutter across gripped knuckles. Autumn chill reddens my cheeks, flying down Fleet Street. Suits stride the pavement, flashing a glance. Blonde hair, skirt flying – better luck next time boys!

17:24 THE VISITOR: ANGELA MEYER (2012)

It is too late for the visitor to realise her mistake, stuck at the bottom of one-way escalators, rushed along by the crowd. The weight of the earth, buildings, sky all press upon her chest. She tries to breathe, to keep her suitcase away from feet that know their business. Picca*diddly*, she thinks, that's what we called it in Monopoly.

17:46 PATIENCE IS A VIRTUE: MARK LEWIS (2013)

The crowds stopped. No room to move. The barriers were closed. Men in fluorescent jackets watched from the gangways. The transport police held a man up against the wall, their dog pawing him. A voice spoke over the tannoy: "This is a public announcement. Stay calm. There is no cause for concern." It was going to be a long night.

Twitcher on the tracks

Commuters going out of London swish past birds that predate humans; they clunker within metres of luminous kingfishers; and only when their Pendolino trains have shrugged off the suburbs will they come close to the top speed of the capital's fastest residents – peregrine falcons. All of this missed as passengers withdraw behind books and newspapers, lose themselves in the screen of their smartphone or the sound of their favourite MP3 tracks.

Heading west, you'll be carried in from Paddington past the reservoirs north of Staines. Along the water's edge there will be swans and ducks. Some crested grebe will perform their mating dance, all as oblivious to the rattling carriages and the rattled passengers are to the watery world outside the windows.

To the north, Hertfordshire's leafy fields and woods, echoing to the sound of cooing pigeons and cawing crows, quickly become entangled in mosaics of gardens. This is the domain of the robins, blackbirds and starlings all competing for space at the bird tables or the scrappy ends of gardens where brambles, creepers and grass cuttings harbour dunnocks, foxes and muntjac deer. The occasional hedgehog will still be found nosing around for a snack and exploring gaps in the fences.

Trains out of Liverpool Street roll through the marshy flood plains of Walthamstow. Changing climate has brought bright white little egrets to its watercourses. They stand out a mile against the greens, greys and browns of the reeds and willows. Less obvious but bigger are the grey herons. Standing motionless like guards. They're waiting for food to come to them on the shallow banks. If it fails they'll leap to the air and flap lazily off to other watery stretches like the River Lea or the mighty Thames to seek out eels or fish missed by the greedy cormorants. All look like small pterodactyls, with their curvy necks, long beaks and sleek wings.

Exiting via the east, running parallel with the Thames, the trains clatter through brownfield wastelands where Ford once dominated or the docks echoed to machinery. Now the wastelands host dwindling numbers of black redstarts and the tall and abandoned industrial buildings lend themselves to nesting peregrines. They'll perch on ledges, surveying the landscape and twice a day will take to the air to search for food, like a pigeon or a ring necked parakeet. Similar to an enemy fighter pilot, they dive on prey from above, capable of speeds of more than 200 mph, they rarely return to their nest without food.

Fenchurch Street is like a larder for peregrines, and is full of pigeons waddling through the fast moving feet of commuters. London Bridge now lies at the foot of the Shard. On the fringes, cutting through the rumble and roar of London life, you'll hear the chatter of house sparrows. Once the capital's most common birds, we've lost seven out of every ten sparrows in London over the past fifteen years. Now they're dwindling to scattered and isolated colonies. Time is eroding their numbers. Hope is literally

blooming though, after months of research led to the growing of wildflower meadows. Like those in the Olympic Park, these swathes of colour, nectar and scent will increase seed and insects for birds like sparrows to eat. The sidings of the underground are linear parks, now managed as scrub where sparrow food and sparrows can thrive. All that's needed to close the loop, is for Londoners to join the party and sow some seeds, grow a hedge, leave some long grass to give homes to London's oldest residents – its wildlife.

Tim Webb, RSPB Officer

The twitcher's checklist

Tim Webb, Royal Society for the Protection of Birds, London

☐ House sparrows – along sidings and at stations

☐ Starlings – overhead and around stations

☐ Crows and rooks – treetops and parks

☐ Wood pigeons – arable fields, woodland and sometimes on trains

☐ Little egrets – waterways, reservoirs, marshes

☐ Swans and ducks – rivers, ponds, lakes

☐ Swifts – screaming overhead between June and September

☐ Sparrowhawks – hunting along sidings

I have surely seen the affliction of my people which are in Egypt, and have heard their cry by reason of their taskmasters; for I know their sorrows.

Exodus 3:7

Train tweet

David Grant @DJG_official

People swarming onto this train at London Bridge like its the last chopper out of Saigon #london #commute

Richard Cobb takes the liquid train

Or take the 5:50 from Cannon Street, a different regiment, and a different, but equally uniform sex, but still in the mutually recognisable uniforms (Tunbridge Wells was a place where clothes called to clothes, cutting out words and greetings) of Boyne Park, Molyneux Park, Frant Road, Warwick Park (but not Broadwater Down, which would go by road self-driven or chauffeur-driven): dark blue three-piece pin-stripe, Van Heusen (semi-stiff) shirts in blue-and-white or red-and-white stripes (some of the stripes a bit on the wide side, not quite the thing, maybe not Molyneux Park), protruding cuffs held by (discreet) gold or silver cuff-links, polka-dot ties, white on blue or white on red silk handkerchiefs to match, or silk Old School ties (Lancing, Tonbridge, Cranford, Haileybury, Eastbourne, Radley, Sutton Valence, Merchant Taylors, Bradfield), or those of the Blue Mantles Cricket Club, plus the regulation accompanying kit: bowler, rolled-up umbrella, battered and smudged *Daily Telegraph*, despatch case in pale pigskin (but not too pale) bought at the leather shop, Pullan's, on the London Road – sandy moustache optional, but not obligatory, voices loud, fruity, throaty, wheezy, laugh penetrating, forced, horsey, neighing, offensive, jokes unsubtle, risqué, predictable; stance: standing at the bar, facing mirror-image: faces, pink to scarlet, touches of mauve, eyes pale-blue and watery, eyebrows sandy and curling in little horns, at the ends; activity: drinking double-gin-and-its, large whisky-and-sodas. The 5:50 was the liquid train – 6 to 7 doubles between Cannon Street and the Wells – and so one that sought out the hard core of the 25 to 55 alcoholic age-group.
From Still Life: Sketches from a Tunbridge Wells Childhood *(1983)*

John Galsworthy heads home

Soames used the Underground again in going home. The fog was worse than ever at Sloane Square station. Through the still, thick blur, men groped in and out; women, very few, grasped their reticules to their bosoms and handkerchiefs to their mouths; crowned with the weird excrescence of the driver, haloed by a vague glow of lamplight that seemed to drown in vapour before it reached the pavement, cabs loomed dim-shaped ever and again, and discharged citizens bolting like rabbits to their burrows.

And these shadowy figures, wrapped each in his own little shroud of fog, took no notice of each other. In the great warren, each rabbit for himself, especially those clothed in this more expensive fur, who, afraid of carriages on foggy days, are driven underground.
From "The Man of Property": The Forsyte Saga, *Vol. I (1906)*

MY COMMUTE: THE DISRUPTED

Posted by Catherine Rogan on Reddit.com,
Waterloo to Woking, 18th December 2012

Left Waterloo at 17:39. Our train came to a very abrupt halt just outside Clapham – so abrupt that I initially thought we had hit someone. We pulled into Clapham Junction and the guard announced that someone had been hit by a train. There were lots of tuts and grumbling, then a young woman said "just before Christmas, how sad" and everyone who had been tutting looked a bit sheepish. The guard announced that he didn't know how long we would be but thought we might be a while, so he opened the doors so people could get off and stretch their legs. We sat around for about 20 mins, then they announced the train wouldn't move before 19:00. People were making small talk!!! Just after 19:00 the guard announced that as there were trains behind us that needed the platform, we all had to get off the train. We did this. No other trains stopped at the platform. There were no staff about at Clapham. There were announcements but the announcements were just to tell us they didn't know what was happening. Several trains went through without stopping.

Later I went up to the footbridge area where there was one man from South West Trains fielding questions from lots of very angry people. He didn't have useful suggestions about getting to Woking. The boards were showing the next train to Woking as being 00:20. I didn't have any mobile signal at all so I couldn't follow @SWTrains tweets (which are usually quite useful) and I couldn't call my partner (I couldn't find a payphone, either). I didn't have 20p to use the loo and there were no seats (I am recovering from a broken ankle and 3h of standing up did it no good – I saw two heavily pregnant women who almost certainly needed a sit down and the loo more than me). I saw a few people actually in tears – if I'd have been picking up my son or hadsomething important to be home for I would have been in tears as well.

From out of nowhere, the boards on Platform 9 announced a train coming, and it was going to Woking! The excitement! The train did indeed stop, and we all crowded round the doors. The doors didn't open and the train drove off!! This happened three times with different trains. The third time people were seriously getting angry, one man was stood on a bench taking a picture of (I assume) the staff in their staff room through a window. Then they announced that Platform 9 was closed and we should go back to Waterloo. Once I did that I was lucky in that as I got off the train they were announcing a train to Woking, which I got on. It was very overcrowded but it got me back to Woking.

I understand that the delays are inevitable, clearing up a body that has been hit by a train is a horrible task (especially if the train was at speed, I had a friend whose brother was a funeral director, he said if a train hits you at speed the police have to walk up the track for a mile picking bits up) and I think they had to turn the power off on some of the lines. What pissed me off was the lack of staff and of info, and the fact that trains clearly were going south, just not stopping at Clapham (some were rammed, but some weren't).

A person under a train happens with sad regularity and every time it causes absolute chaos. An American visitor thought it odd that we have a pre-recorded announcement for "person hit by a train", she thought it wasn't something that would happen enough to have a standard announcement.

I'm home now, and I have wine. I feel most sorry for the person's family, and for the driver of the train, all of whom have had a far, far shittier evening than me.

Commuter Workout

Kathryn Miller, exercise expert, personal trainer, massage therapist,
ex-commuter, www.bodybalancemassagetherapy.co.uk

Discreet exercises designed to be performed in very limited space to transform the weary homeward journey.

Try to hold each stretch for 20–30 seconds.

1) Wrist Circling

Circle each hand ten times to the left and ten to the right. This will help mobilise the arm and wrist flexor and extensor muscles and the small carpal bones of the wrist.

2) Pectorals

Bend arm against wall/partition of train, elbow at shoulder height, fingers pointing to train roof. Gently step forwards with the foot nearest the elevated arm. Feel the pectoral stretch. Repeat both sides. Will stretch muscles including the *pectoralis major, pectoralis minor* and *anterior deltoid*.

3) Forearm Flexors and Extensors Stretch

Holding arm straight, point fingers upwards to stretch the flexors (on lower forearm) and downwards to stretch the extensors (on upper forearm). Will stretch muscles including the *extensor digitorum, extensor carpi radialis longus* and *flexor carpi ulnaris*.

4) Thumb Stretch

Stick thumb out on one hand, use other hand to pull thumb downwards to stretch the palm. Will stretch muscles including *adductor pollicis* and *flexor pollicis longus*.

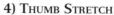

5) Chest Stretch

Clasp hands together behind head, pull elbows and hands backwards to feel pectorals and deltoids stretch. Will stretch muscles including the *pectoralis major, pectoralis minor, anterior deltoid* and *serratus anterior*.

6) Neck Flexion Stretch

Standing with back straight, look down towards floor to feel stretch in back of neck and upper back muscles. Will stretch muscles including the *semispinalis* muscles, *levator scapulae* and *longissimus capitis*.

7) Neck Extension Stretch

Keeping back straight, look upwards to train ceiling to feel front of neck muscles stretch. Will stretch muscles including *platysma* and *sternocleidomastoid*.

8) Lateral Neck Stretch

Keeping back straight, tip head to side, ear towards shoulder, ensuring the shoulder doesn't rise upwards towards ceiling. Will stretch muscles including *trapezius, sternocleidomastoid* and *levator scapulae*.

9) Rotation Stretch

Reach both hands towards train ceiling and rotate upper body to the left. Repeat to the right side. Will stretch muscles including *quadratus lumborum,* the obliques, the *multifidi* and the *longissimus thoracis*.

10) Ankle Circling, and Toe and Heel Raises

Standing straight, rotate foot 10 times to the left then 10 times to the right. Repeat for other foot. Next, raise one heel off the ground keeping toe on the floor, repeat 10 times. Do the same for toe, keeping heel on ground. Will stretch lower leg muscles including *gastrocnemius* and mobilise the small tarsal bones of the ankle.

Timeline VII

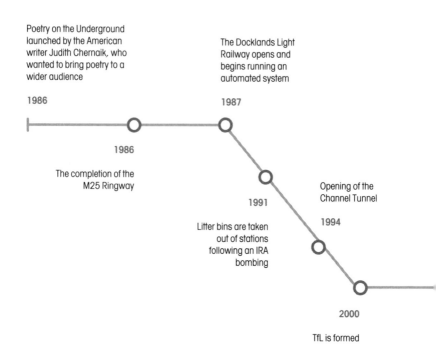

Poetry on the Underground launched by the American writer Judith Chernaik, who wanted to bring poetry to a wider audience

1986

The Docklands Light Railway opens and begins running an automated system

1987

1986

The completion of the M25 Ringway

Opening of the Channel Tunnel

1994

1991

Litter bins are taken out of stations following an IRA bombing

2000

TfL is formed

Oyster Card is
launched

July 2003

Metropolitan Police
shoot dead Jean
Charles De Menezes in
Stockwell Tube station
after mistakenly
misidentifying him as a
terrorist suspect just
two weeks after the
London bombings

22 July 2005

Opened alcohol is
banned on Tubes

2008

7 July 2005

Four terrorist bombers
detonate bombs
targeting civilians on
public transport during
the London morning
rush-hour. Three
bombs explode on
Underground trains;

a fourth is detonated
on a No. 30 bus in
Tavistock Square. 52
civilians are killed
along with the four
bombers themselves,
and over 700 more
are injured.

2007

St Pancras
International Station is
opened and begins
running services from
London to Paris Gare
Du Nord station

8

SERENADE

Evening Star, you bring in all things

Scattered wide by the dawn

You bring the goat back to the meadow

As the mother brings back the child...

There's a choice: linger, or head for home. In spring and autumn the violet hour is the commuting hour. In those seasons the sun goes down without fire, leaving behind a cool tinge in the sky. Sappho tells us how "sorrowful" Eirana with her "blackened onyx eyes" gathers at dusk the flowers and "brings together all the dazzling dawn has put asunder."

Whence Eliot and his "violet hour" in "The Fire Sermon" and his "violet air" in "What the Thunder Said", both sections of *The Waste Land* (1922). Eliot provided notes to the allusion: "This may not appear as exact as Sappho's lines, but I had in mind a 'longshore' or 'dory' fisherman, who returns at nightfall." The violet hue is liturgical, perhaps associated with baptism, possibly a reference to the Perilous Chapel in Jessie L Weston's *From Ritual to Romance*, through which the knight must pass in order to obtain the Grail – a portal or baptism. The "bats with baby faces" of "The Fire Sermon" could happily hang in the Perilous Chapel. The violet margin of the day tests mettle and mood. Eliot's twilight sees the sun going down on civilisation...

Where the morning is structured, the evening is looser. Each evening has its own taste. Monday is eager and expeditious. Tuesday is neutral. Wednesday is a watershed. Thursday – with the weekend close – sees workers drinking heavily and late, collapsing onto night trains to sleep and flirt. Friday can be perfunctory, the weekend too good to delay.

For those who leave London during the peak rush home, the ride can be even more cramped than in the morning. For a reason beyond all reason, most offices release their aircon-dried, clock watching, worry-worn staff between 5 and 6 o'clock. As is natural, everyone leaves as soon as they can (those who voluntarily work overtime for no pay are new, worried, keen, naïve, friendless). The great mass of workers begins to shuffle and prepare at five minutes to the prescribed hour. The escapist may feel the stabbing stares from managers and jobsworths, but still he weaves through the desks, and once on the street his pace picks up. He is fired up for Cannon Street, he hikes determinedly towards Moorgate.

The ride is shaky, heated, keen. Passengers gather thoughts in the secular

"Out in the birdsinging suburbs, the evening stretches out its shadows"

compline of the carriage. At the other end it's all joy. Out in the birdsinging suburbs, the evening stretches out its shadows. Only three gauntlets to run: the local winestore; the small super-maket; picking up the kids.

As late as the 1950s, a million garden gates opened and closed and a million wives stood on doorsteps, in evening dress or gardening gloves. Scotch was poured on rocks and home, gendered, was where the heart was. In the 2010s, two people stumble in around the same time, or two parents and two children, or a trio of thirtysomething flat-sharers. Still, the evening is for homely rituals. The domestic confessions, the summing-up of the day's chaos, the main meal of the day – no sandwiches now, no latte, no queue, but plenty of wine and beer, and conversation, and television, and a suburban song as romantic in its way as any balcony serenade.

Or, the city and its night: the shops close, offices close, light dims. Virginia Woolf, in her 1927 essay *Street Haunting*, celebrates the shuttered-down centre:

"With no thought of buying, the eye is sportive and generous; it creates; it adorns; it enhances." After the blindness of the morning's arrival, now the com-muter – delaying his role – can see, hear, explore. London is revealed to be more than a working machine, in fact it no longer wears that suit at all.

The commuter, too, puts away his work self and becomes theatregoer, rock fan, AA member, pub legend, hobbyist, club member, party animal, restaurant critic, lone wolf, free – at last he owns the city, belongs to it, desires it. Little won-der there is so much clamour and cele-bration in the metropolis as the evening shifts to night; it's people waking up at last, fighting the deep fatigue of the day.

Between as early as eight o' clock and around midnight, vapours of vodka and ale, expired pasties and sweated curries fill the trains that snake out of the terminals. In a single carriage there might be a man arrived at retirement age, boozed up and warm from pats on the back after his last day at the office and, sat beside him, a 20-year-old intern, joyful at being taken out by his new bosses after his first four days and now, inebriated, wondering if he committed any *faux pas*. Women sit on men's knees, enemies flirt and make promises, opera goers from Richmond jostle with electricians from Łódz, gym-fit builders brush up against soft-bellied bankers.

And if you miss those trains, you enter a new dimension: after another very bad party in a north London suburb, a party at which the food was pretentious and otiose and the drink plentiful but cheap, I left, alone, and stumbled semiconsciously through streets of high sodium-lit houses and found myself, like a dumb beast, on a desolate tube train to Waterloo. There the internal programming put me onto a train heading southwest, found a seat not filled with annoying conversation, and then shut down. I woke up when the train stopped in a dark and apparently rural place, many miles past my intended destination, and jumped through the doors onto a bare platform.

Only one other passenger had alighted. I asked him where we were. He read the platform sign. Effingham Junction. He said he'd fallen asleep. I said I'd done the same. He said he was from Wigan. I told him I was originally from a village near St Helens. We were equally useless when it came to determining the way home. We tried the one taxi number printed on the station's local information board. They hung up on us. The pie-eater, who said he'd been seeing his ex-missus in Clapham, decided to walk back to London…following the tracks. He must have imagined there was a similar dearth of traffic on the SWT line as on the Wigan Wallgate–Rainford diesel line, and I suppose he was flattened by a Dorset-bound express some time around 1:30am.

I decided to use the constellations, natural and man-made. I looked in the sky and thought I saw a glow: London. Then I walked out of the station and turned left. I finished up sleeping in a bus shelter, meeting badgers, and catching the Polish worker bus back to Kingston upon Thames sometime after dawn.

The sleeper is the last phase of the raucous night. He is the dregs. The loser. The rite of sleeping on the train is one of the many baptisms that make you a London commuter. I'm glad I had my moment in the starlight ∎

Schubert's *Ständchen*

My song beckons softly to you
Through the night;
Down to the silent wood
My love, come to me!

The tree-tops whisper
In the light of the moon;

Don't be afraid, my love,
No-one will spy on us.

Can you hear the nightingales?
Oh! They beckon to you
With their sweet-sounding song,
They beckon to you for me,

They understand the yearning I feel,
They know love's torture,
With their silvery notes

They touch every soft heart.

Let them touch yours, too,
Sweet love: hear my plea!
Trembling I await you,
Come,
Bring me bliss!

Ludwig Rellstab (1828)

MY COMMUTE: THE ESCAPIST

Jessica Baldwin, Tottenham Court Road London to Welwyn Garden City, 2012–present

I stopped living in London the second I realised I had become a Londoner.

I realised this, as many people do, during the infamous London commute; a case of survival of the fittest.

I had gone from the country girl skipping through the tunnels admiring the posters uttering, "No, please, after me", to a one-woman tank storming down escalators, tut-tutting at the dawdlers and rolling my eyes at tourists as I dislocated shoulders whilst ramming myself through the bleeping Tube doors. Well, how could I possibly wait for the next Tube? It wasn't due for a whole minute!

Nowadays, having abandoned the big smoke, my commute is from leafy Hertfordshire, and despite the elongated duration, the commute home makes it all worthwhile. After a furious sprint, leap-frogging pushchairs and hurdling over amateurs, I make it to the train, literally the light at the end of the tunnel. As the train pulls out of hectic King's Cross I feel the Londoner ebb out of me. The black tunnels and building works are gradually replaced by lush fields, leafy trees and relaxed locals wondering why I look so dishevelled. Every evening, as I reach my chocolate box village and stare out lovingly at the local dawdlers and tourists, a smile creeps onto my face as everything falls into perspective. London is a state of mind.

Sappho's Fragment 104

Evening Star, you bring in all things

Scattered wide by the dawn

You bring the goat back to the meadow

As the mother brings back the child...

Evening Star, I think you are

The fairest of all the stars.

Fragments 104a and 104b (7th–6th century BC), trans. Chris Moss

Eating out in 1884

*Advertisement for a restaurant at 27 High Street, Islington,
produced by T. EVANS & Co. Printers, 327 Goswell Road, London, E.C.*

CHOP OR STEAK	**8d**
ROAST BEEF	**6d**
ROAST LEG MUTTON	**7d**
ROAST PORK & APPLE SAUCE	**7d**
STEAK PUDDING	**4d**
VEGETABLES	**1d & 2d**
PASTRY & PUDDING	**1d & 2d**
TEA PER CUP	**1½ d**
TEA PER POT	**2d**
COFFEE OR COCOA	**1d & 1½ d**
SAUSAGE & MASHED POTATOES	**2½ d**
BACON	**2d**
EGGS	**1½ d**
STEWED TRIPE & ONIONS	**4d & 6d**

FROM 6–12 PM

BUNS, SCONES, COLD MEAT & MINERAL WATERS.

BEDS 1/- PER NIGHT

Repetition

Commuter – one who spends his life

In riding to and from his wife;

A man who shaves and takes a train

And then rides back to shave again.

"Commuter" (1929) by EB White

The evening exodus

After leaving the office I would travel either to Sloane Square or to Liverpool Street to have a drink in the station buffet. In the whole extension of the Underground system those two stations are, as far as I've been able to discover, the only ones which have bars actually on the platform. The whole concept of the tube station platform bar excited me… Drinking there between six and seven in the shifting crowd of rush-hour travellers, one could feel on one's shoulders as a curiously soothing yoke the weariness of toiling London, that blank released tiredness after work which can somehow console even the bored, even the frenzied. The coming and departing rattle of the trains, the drifting movement of the travellers, their arrival, their waiting, their vanishing forever presented a mesmeric and indeed symbolic fresco: so many little moments of decision, so many little finalities, the constant wrenching of texture, the constant destruction of cells which shifts and ages the lives of men and of universes.

From A Word Child *(1975) by Iris Murdoch*

"From the Suburbs"

Dollie Radford (1895)

It rushes home, our own express,
So cheerfully, no one would guess
The weight it carries

Of tired husbands, back from town,
For each of whom, in festal gown,
A fond wife tarries.

For each of whom a better half,
At even, serves the fatted calf,
In strange disguises,

At anxious boards of all degree,
Down to the simple "egg at tea,"
Which love devises.

For whom all day, disconsolate,
Deserted villas have to wait,
Detached and Semi-

Barred by their own affairs, which are
As hard to pass through as the far
Famed Alpine Gemmi.

Sometimes as I at leisure roam,
Admiring my suburban home,
I wonder sadly

If men will always come and go
In these vast numbers, to and fro,
So fast and madly.

I muse on what the spell can be,
Which causes this activity:
Who of our Sages

The potent charm has meted out
To tall and thin, to short and stout,
Of varying ages.

I think, when other fancy flags,
The magic lies within the bags
Which journey ever

In silent, black mysterious ways,
With punctual owners, all their days
And fail them never.

In some perhaps sweet flowers lie,
Sweet flowers which shape a destiny
To pain or pleasure,

Or lady's glove, or ringlet bright,
Or many another keepsake light,
Which true knights treasure.

May be – may be – Romance is rife,
Despite our busy bustling life,
And rules us gaily,

And shows no sign of weariness,
But in our very own express,
Does travel daily.

London streets

The hour should be the evening and the season winter, for in winter the champagne brightness of the air and the sociability of the streets are grateful. We are not then taunted as in the summer by the longing for shade and solitude and sweet airs from the hayfields. The evening hour, too, gives us the irresponsibility which darkness and lamplight bestow. We are no longer quite ourselves. As we step out of the house on a fine evening between four and six, we shed the self our friends know us by and become part of that vast republican army of anonymous trampers, whose society is so agreeable after the solitude of one's own room. For there we sit surrounded by objects which perpetually express the oddity of our own temperaments and enforce the memories of our own experience.

…How beautiful a London street is then, with its islands of light, and its long groves of darkness, and on one side of it perhaps some tree-sprinkled, grass-grown space where night is folding herself to sleep naturally…

From Street Haunting: A London Adventure *(1927) by Virginia Woolf*

OK, Commuter

Commuters are also, can't help it, computers, constantly counting the minutes. This can be boring. But then, a final flourish of seemingly random perversity, the last train at 23:37. (The last train is more like a party that's lost its energy. Most of the guests are half asleep and the ticket collector, a caring butler, politely asks you your station; he will come and wake you up.)
From Commuting in Restless Cities *(2010) by Rachel Bowlby*

Carriage kisses

In the railway carriage, I once more clasped my Lilian in my arms, and found to my great delight that she was what I should call a natural kisser, revelling in long-drawn-out caresses of the mouth. Her lips seemed to weld themselves to mine, and I am sure that my dove-like osculation and the touch of my throat, ears and eyes gave her as much pleasure as a girl could feel.

"Your kisses make me crazy!" or: "Your mouth drives me mad!" were two of her favourite phrases as, when shivering with lasciviousness, she would tear herself from my embrace, only to put up her brilliant mouth over and over again a moment afterwards.

There was no doubt that she had no physical repugnance to me, for it often occurs that a woman thinks she would like a man, and when he at last takes her in his arms, something about him, his odour, his skin, his manner of embracing, his breath, nay, the merest trifle, sometimes rudely dispels all the delight of being clasped to my breast, and my lips pleased her as hers did me…

My hands wandered all over her body, pressing her luxuriant posteriors, her thighs, which I found of proper size, her arms, hands, and neck, and I exclaimed:

"I know that Lilian returns the love I have felt for her for two years, although I am twice her age. I am happy now and care for naught else!"

And it was true. I was drunk with love, desire, lust, passion, call it what you will.

I made her unfasten her jacket, and sought to press her breasts, but there were only two little faintly-developed hillocks. Her cloth dress was closely fastened under her arm with hooks and eyes. "You hurt me," she said, as I feverishly moulded her little bosom.

"I love to hurt you. I love to think that you are mine to do with as I choose, to make you suffer, if I so will it, and I'll squeeze your tiny breasts until you wince with pain."

"They are small," she retorted, laughingly, "but they are firm."

From Suburban Souls: The Erotic Psychology of a Man and a Maid *(1901), written by a 43-year-old stockbroker known only as "Jacky S"*

Eating out in 2013
Set menu at Bluebird, a "Modern British" restaurant in Chelsea

Gazpacho – San Marzano tomato, basil
Foie gras and chicken liver parfait – Earl Grey jelly, toasted sourdough
Butter lettuce salad – chives, tarragon, champagne vinaigrette

Pan-roast Loch Duart salmon – brown shrimps, leeks, horseradish sauce
Slow-cooked pork belly – spring onion mash
English pea risotto – pea, mint and herb salad

Mashed potatoes £3.50,
French fries £3.50,
Buttered spinach £4.00, Steamed broccoli £4.00,
Mac and cheese £4.00,
Dressed leaves £4.50,
Garden peas, lettuce and onion £4.50,
Tomato salad and onion £5.00

Sticky toffee pudding – banana, clotted cream
Yogurt panna cotta – vanilla poached strawberries
Tiramisu – chocolate, amaretti

2 courses £20
or
3 courses £25
with a glass
of Garganega
or a glass of Barbera

The bus home

At the corner of Oxford Circus Rosabel bought a bunch of violets, and that was practically the reason why she had so little tea – for a scone and a boiled egg and a cup of cocoa at Lyons are not ample sufficiency after a hard day's work in a millinery establishment. As she swung on to the step of the Atlas 'bus, grabbed her skirt with one hand and clung to the railing with the other, Rosabel thought she would have sacrificed her soul for a good dinner – roast duck and green peas, chestnut stuffing, pudding with brandy sauce – something hot and strong and filling. She sat down next to a girl very much her own age who was reading *Anna Lombard* in a cheap, paper-covered edition, and the rain had tear-spattered the pages.

Rosabel looked out of the windows; the street was blurred and misty, but light striking on the panes turned their dullness to opal and silver, and the jewellers' shops seen through this, were fairy palaces. Her feet were horribly wet, and she knew the bottom of her skirt and petticoat would be coated with black, greasy mud. There was a sickening smell of warm humanity – it seemed to be oozing out of everybody in the 'bus – and everybody had the same expression, sitting so still, staring in front of them. How many times had she read these advertisements – "Sapolio Saves Time, Saves Labour" – "Heinz's Tomato Sauce" – and the inane, annoying dialogue between doctor and judge concerning the superlative merits of "Lamplough's Pyretic Saline."

She glanced at the book which the girl read so earnestly, mouthing the words in a way that Rosabel detested, licking her first finger and thumb each time that she turned the page. She could not see very clearly; it was something about a hot, voluptuous night, a band playing, and a girl with lovely, white shoulders. Oh, Heavens! Rosabel stirred suddenly and unfastened the two top buttons of her coat … she felt almost stifled. Through her half-closed eyes the whole row of people on the opposite seat seemed to resolve into one fatuous, staring face.

And this was her corner. She stumbled a little on her way out and lurched against the girl next her. "I beg your pardon," said Rosabel, but the girl did not even look up. Rosabel saw that she was smiling as she read.

From The Tiredness of Rosabel *(1908) by Katherine Mansfield*

Home

After my work in the City, I like to be at home.
What's the good of a home, if you are never in it?
From Diary of a Nobody *(1892) by*
George Grossmith and Weedon Grossmith

THE CITY GENT – STRIPPED

8. SLIPPERS

A scotch on the rocks served on arrival. It's a nostalgic image, a '70s sitcom scene. Perhaps the liquor is now a good Pinot Grigio from Marks, or a Margaux from Majestic. And the evening's eschatology: the tie cast off, the belt unbuckled, the braces unclipped, the handkerchief checked and stored, the briefcase slotted into that narrow space between the bureau for the bills and bank stuff and the telephone table, and the bowler and the brolly…well, there must be a few of these out in the far-flung suburbs, where the oldest gents sit reflecting on time spent in a different kind of City long before Black Monday. Stockinged feet, and perhaps pyjamas and a robe, and the mobile switched off and the iPad put to charge, and then the

slippers come out and at last he is neither City nor Gent, but just his name and his bedroom-bound self. The scotch melting, watery. Still a caricature, still old-fashioned, and not still at all, but tapping a hand and a foot, on edge, commuting in his head from home to office, back and forth, not sure which end is the right one.

Décor for dinner parties

Have you ever reflected that the furnishing of your drawing room will have its effect upon the conversation of your guests? It certainly will. Put some people in a room of the commonplace kind, and they inevitably become commonplace in their conversation. Meet somewhere else where by accident or design a few odds and ends of individual character have crept into the room and they positively sparkle.

The Art and Craft of Homemaking (1913) by Edward William Gregory

To one who has been long in city pent

To one who has been long in city pent,

'Tis very sweet to look into the fair

And open face of heaven – to breathe a prayer

Full in the smile of the blue firmament.

Who is more happy, when, with heart's content,

Fatigued he sinks into some pleasant lair

Of wavy grass, and reads a debonair

And gentle tale of love and languishment?

Returning home at evening, with an ear

Catching the notes of Philomel – an eye

Watching the sailing cloudlet's bright career,

He mourns that day so soon has glided by:

E'en like the passage of an angel's tear

That falls through the clear ether silently.

John Keats (1817)

Last Train to Dagenham

I'll be on the last train to Dagenham
I've been drinking in a pub up west
I'm looking for the sign that says this is the District line
and I'm gonna catch the alky express

I'll be on the last train to Dagenham
With all the other ravers, drunk and stoned
Empty cans of Tenants Super rattle at my feet
And I'm wondering if I'll ever make it home

'Coz I've drunk the dole and I've drunk my flatmate's rent
he'll never speak to me again, if I don't get some money sent

'Coz I've drunk the dole and I've drunk my flatmate's rent
he'll never speak to me again, if I don't get some money sent

I'll be on the last train to Dagenham
Shattered, worn out, knackered, shagged and tired
But if I miss my stop, I know I'll have a bloody long walk home
So I'm trying to keep my eyes open wide

I'll be on the last train to Dagenham
I'll be on the last train to Dagenham
I'll be on the last train to Dagenham

From the album Guilty as Charged *(1994) by Cock Sparrer*

Sleep: the solution

1. OPTIMISE YOUR SLEEP TIME

Calculate backwards from the time you need to leave your home to establish
what time you need to go to bed. If you have to leave at 8am, deduct the time you
need for breakfast, the time you take to wash and dress, 7.5 hours for sleep, add
10 minutes for wake up and 15 minutes for falling asleep. You have your official
bedtime.

2. RELEASE RESIDUAL STRESS

All jobs come with their quota of stress. Most people I meet carry home that
stress and mull it over in the hours of darkness. To reduce stress and deal with
the following day's potential "anxiety hangover", do the following: build a
15-minute walk from the station/car park/bus-stop into your schedule – this will
help you clear your head and give you fresh air and, in summer, daylight, and
you'll sleep better. Write a list of things you need to achieve tomorrow, put it in
your bag and close the bag. Talk through difficult meetings with a partner or
friend – try to devise three action points to move the situation forward.

3. KEEP YOUR ENERGY LEVELS STABLE

An adequate breakfast enables you to perform more efficiently, reduces your
chances of putting on weight – and a healthy weight improves sleep. The "break"
in your "fast" is part of a natural cycle: your body likes carbs in the morning to
give it a good energy boost. Adding low-glycaemic index foods (wholegrain
cereals, nuts, fresh fruit) helps release these slowly and you won't feel you need a
sugar fix to give you a mid-morning zing. If you balance this with some protein,
studies show it will improve your ability to multi-task. Caffeinated coffee is fine –
it improves alertness. Make lunch protein-rich and alcohol-free to reduce blood
sugars and help avoid a mid-afternoon energy dip. Overall, make sure your diet
contains sufficient amounts of iron (from green leafy vegetables, whole grains
and cereals as well as red meat) as iron prevents daytime sleepiness. Vitamin
C-rich fruit helps iron absorption.
Adapted from Sound Asleep: The Expert Guide to Sleeping Well *(2013)*
by Dr. Chris Idzikowsi

Timeline VIII

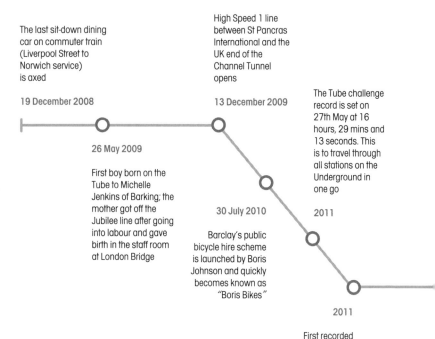

The last sit-down dining
car on commuter train
(Liverpool Street to
Norwich service)
is axed

19 December 2008

High Speed 1 line
between St Pancras
International and the
UK end of the
Channel Tunnel
opens

13 December 2009

The Tube challenge
record is set on
27th May at 16
hours, 29 mins and
13 seconds. This
is to travel through
all stations on the
Underground in
one go

2011

26 May 2009

First boy born on the
Tube to Michelle
Jenkins of Barking; the
mother got off the
Jubilee line after going
into labour and gave
birth in the staff room
at London Bridge

30 July 2010

Barclay's public
bicycle hire scheme
is launched by Boris
Johnson and quickly
becomes known as
"Boris Bikes"

2011

First recorded
successful proposal
on the Tube in
November (Adam King
to Lucy Rodgers)

The New Bus for London – inspired by the old Routemaster – begins operating on Route 24 between Hampstead Heath and Pimlico (prototypes started running on the No. 3 route in February 2012)

The controversial High Speed Rail Link between London and Birmingham is set for completion with Phase 2 links to the north including Manchester and Leeds set for completion in 2032

TUC study shows average daily commute for London is 75 minutes per day

November 2012

22 June 2013

2026

30 January 2013

2018

Prince Charles (with Camilla, Duchess of Cornwall) rides the Tube for the first time in 33 years to celebrate 150 years of The London Underground

Crossrail to open linking Berkshire to Buckinghamshire via Greater London to Essex

9

DEPARTURES

And there was the ferryman just as Virgil

And Dante had seen him. He looked at us coldly

And his eyes were dead and his hands on the oar

Were black with obols and varicose veins

Marbled his calves and he said to us coldly:

If you want to die you will have to pay for it.

Louis MacNeice

...and the angels of God ascending and descending upon the Son of Man   *John 1:51*

In America, which used to be the future, commuting ordinarily means being seated in a car, in gridlock, moving very slowly or not at all. China, multitudinously lacking in imagination, has in a single generation taken a great leap backward from the cheap, efficient bicycle to a national obsession with car ownership. Brussels and Antwerp are numbers one and two in the traffic jam stakes, with Los Angeles crawling in as an unsurprising third. São Paulo currently holds the unofficial world record for traffic jams: 112 miles is the reported average and 183 miles is possible on a bad day. Brazil's biggest city is also famous for its helicopter commuters; there are more than 400 helipads and 500-odd choppers ferrying groups of up to six passengers across the sprawl. Every week, more than 1,100 aeroplane flights ply the 223 miles betweeen Con-

gonhas, São Paulo's domestic airport, and Santos Dumont in Rio de Janeiro. Tokyo Haneda operates commuter flights to Fukuoka, Osaka and Sapporo, transporting more than 20 million people every year. Sydney-Melbourne, Barcelona-Madrid, Mumbai-Delhi, Seoul-Jeju: the flying commute is becoming the norm. At the other extreme, Copenhagen has 250 miles of bike lanes ("to Copenhagenise" is to become bike-friendly), Curitiba in Brazil and the Colombian capital Bogotá have bus systems that provide the template for public transport-centred big-city developments elsewhere, and Freiburg in Germany and Ghent in Belgium are exploring the utopian notion of car-free city centres.

London, meanwhile, continues to improvise and expand. Crossrail will add a new west-east axis connecting Central London with Maidenhead and Shenfield. The rest is speculation. A projected Crossrail 2 scheme promises an underground railway between Wimbledon and Alexandra Palace with overground connections to Hertford

"Commuters have been destroyed and burned to death on trains"

East and stations across south-west London out to Epsom and Shepperton. The much-discussed High Speed 2 line, far from spreading work and wealth to other parts of England, will almost certainly turn Birmingham into a sort of mega-Barnet and Manchester into Mill Hill North. Heathrow will get a new runway, or not. Ebbsfleet, a fledgling non-burb – when you stop there *en route* to Paris the station has a *Once Upon a Time in the West* feel – will probably become a new-new town.

The system that binds all this together – the commuter network of trains, roads, buses, tubes and bike paths – will be cobbled, patched up, botched.

So much for the future of commuting. These vast, inhuman processes leave behind dead towns, dead lines, dead stations, dead dreams, dead flowers. As the trains evolve, comforts are left behind. No porters, no stationmaster, no food, no loos, no seats. Brands change: London and North Western>London, Midland and Scottish>British Railways>InterCity West Coast >Virgin.

Accidents happen. Improvements and public inquiries. Prices for season tickets rise faster than inflation.

Meanwhile, every commuter must have a final destination. Not the daily one – the terminus, the workplace, the descent into the Tube – but the destiny destination.

There are many possibilities. Retirement is one: the least heroic in the popular imagination, but perhaps the bravest. The ex-commuter suddenly finds himself stranded not on the platform but on the patio or in the loft, waiting for the big night train.

Commuters have been destroyed and burned to death on trains. On the morning of 8th October 1952, a night express train from Perth in Scotland collided with the rear end of a local service travelling from Tring to Euston at Harrow and Wealdstone station. The commuter train was carrying around 800 passengers, busier than normal as the following service had been cancelled.

The collision took place at 8:19am. Seconds later, a third train coming from Euston crashed into the wreckage. In all, 112 died and 340 people were injured, making it the worst railway disaster in peacetime Europe. The Moorgate tube accident of 28th February 1975 that killed 43 and injured 74 took place at 8:46am. The Ladbroke Grove crash of 5th October 1999 took place at 8:08am and killed 31 people and injured more than 500. And of course commuters are ideal targets for terrorists. There is no more potent way to cause panic, pandemonium and death.

There exists, among the amnesiac and credulous, a hope that one day we shall all telecommute. A misnomer of a word, it purports to denote the idea that we can travel to work virtually from a home office or wi-fi-connected café in some beachside location. It's not happening yet and may well turn out to be one of those false promises, rather like the 1970s claims that we would all work less because of computers helping with the Hoovering.

For some, the ultimate destiny involves escape, admitting defeat. I died – as a commuter – in March 2012, but I died trying. Three and a bit years earlier I had taken an office job, which meant I had to commute every day into Waterloo from Surbiton. The people on the platform were archetypes of besuited resignation. Trains came every few minutes – this was a stop on a line with many fast trains from Guildford, Woking, Basingstoke – and they came packed and pungent. Some days I could feel hope bleeding from me. Other days I felt solid and complete. Just the everyday schizophrenia of the commuter I'm sure. But when the sun lit up the smeary windows it seemed like a divine joke.

The end came with an axe. The usual: whisperings, knives in backs, a team of robots taking over the firm to make it web-friendly and then redundancies. I was turned loose.

But perhaps I was always bound to depart in this fashion. Even on empty commuter trains, I had always been the

"For some, the ultimate destiny involves escape, admitting defeat"

one standing up, waiting to get off, looking through the window. I had to accept the facts: I didn't want this any longer. I didn't even want irony, belonging, Betjeman and the romanticisation of the banal. I wanted John Clare:

"Crowded places, I shunned them as noises too rude
And flew to the silence of sweet solitude."

But I still recognise this need as a kind of failure. Taking his cue from Kierkegaard's "leap of faith" – but dropping the "faith" bit – Camus, in *The Myth of Sisyphus,* argues that only when man realises the absurdity of his situation is he free to enjoy life. "One must imagine Sisyphus happy," he writes, recognising that the key difference between a contented soul and a despairing one is attitude, not intelligence.

An acceptance, stoic or otherwise, that the commute is an essential part of life, one of the burdens that allows a worker to own a home, raise a family, pay his bills, buy gifts and be in the world, is an act of dignity. Every age needs its hero and in an era of incon-

stancy, fads, market-driven booms and busts, false freedoms and fake devotions, a sensible, low-key hero is the best we are going to get.

In spite of prejudices from all sides, in spite of all the obstacles and barriers erected by governments and transport planners, in spite of the alarm clock and the ersatz coffee, the commuter comes in every day from Upton, from Sawbridgeworth, from Wye, from Burnt Oak, from Chelmsford, from Theydon Bois, from Herne Hill, from Woking, from Hackney, from Brighton, from Watford, from Wokingham, from Denmark Hill, from Berrylands, from Bitterne, from Box Hill & Westhumble, from Martins Heron, from Princes Risborough, from White City, from Tooting Bec, from Dorking Deepdene, from High Rocks, from Hythe Pier, from Tring, from Virginia Water, from Walton-on-the-Naze, from Surbiton, from Tunbridge Wells, from Thornton Heath, from Elephant & Castle, from Ham, from Harrow, solidly, absurdly, steadfastly, smoothly ∎

The Necropolitan Line

As the population of London and its environs grew in the nineteenth century, older graves were broken up to make space for the newly deceased. By the 1850s, following outbreaks of smallpox, measles and cholera, this solution was shown to be inadequate. Two entrepreneurs, Sir Richard Broun and Richard Sprye, came up with a radical solution: to build a 2,000-acre cemetery 23 miles from London at Brookwood near Woking, with its own dedicated funeral train operating out of Waterloo.

Not everyone backed the scheme. The railway owners were concerned about extra traffic. Bishop of London Charles Blomfield sermonised about the God-given right to a funeral suited to one's social or moral rank: "It may sometimes happen that persons of opposite characters might be carried in the same conveyance. For instance, the body of some profligate spendthrift might be placed in a conveyance with the body of some respectable member of the church, which would shock the feelings of his friends."

Nonetheless, in 1852 Parliament approved the project and the London Necropolis and National Mausoleum Company – later shortened to London Necropolis Company – was established. Two years later the London Necropolis Railway opened. The solution to the objections raised by the Bishop was to provide six classes. In a two-car train there could be one for conformist, i.e. Church of England, funeral parties and another for non-conformists. There were also first-class, second-class or third-class tickets, for living and dead passengers. Each hearse car was split into three sections of four coffin cells each. The LNC even built two stations at Brookwood: graves on the sunny south side of the cemetery would be for Anglicans while the non-conformists would be entombed on the chilly north side.

Between 1854 and 1874, the cemetery averaged only 3,200 burials a year, accounting for less than seven per cent of London's deaths at the time. The service was also abused by the living. A first-class return ticket from Waterloo to Brookwood cost eight shillings on the ordinary London & South-Western Railway's normal service, but only six shillings on Necropolis trains. Golfers travelling from London to West Hill Golf Club, which stood beside Brookwood's grounds, sometimes took advantage of this, dressing up as mourners in order to pay a lower fare.

Despite a low cadaver turnout, the line continued to be used well into the twentieth century. A new station was built at Waterloo in 1902 and operated until 1941, at which point Luftwaffe bombing destroyed first the rolling stock and then parts of the station building.

Ghost stations

QUAINTON ROAD

In the 1890s, the Metropolitan Line's commuter traffic petered out around Aylesbury. Nonetheless the company extended the line deep into rural Buckinghamshire and Oxfordshire, opening stations at Waddesdon, Quainton Road, Brill and Grandborough Road, with a terminus at Verney Junction. If the line was, in broad terms, a democratic endeavour, this Chilterns-crossing extension was a largely feudal enterprise, built because of pressure from the Duke of Buckingham at Wotton and his neighbour Sir Harry Verney, board members on the Aylesbury and Buckingham Railway. The ABR built a six-mile track connecting Aylesbury with Quainton Road, from which ran the Brill Tramway, the Duke's private line to his estate. Bereft of commuters, the Quainton Road/Verney Junction extension was used to transport manure out to the Duke's farms and ferried ducal acquaintances to and from the City. It had two Pullman carriages – *Mayflower* and *Galatea* – and whisky was served *en route* in crystal glasses. Between 1932 and 1936, the extension was closed to passenger trains and in 1947 goods traffic ended too.

WELSH HARP

In 1868, the Midland Railway cut a line through to St Pancras. A popular attraction with day-trippers at the time was the Welsh Harp lake, south of Hendon, formed in 1838 to provide water for the Grand Junction Canal.

In the summer months, it was used by bathers, boaters and anglers and was well served by public houses – one of which provided its name. The area was still largely rural but the railway firm saw the leisure traffic as a potential source of extra revenue and in 1870 opened Welsh Harp station. In 1872 ticket sales were a healthy 22,929 but by 1899 this had fallen to a meagre 8,262, despite improvements at the station and new lines. When the accountants compared other local stations and realised that Welsh Harp sold only one per cent of the tickets sold at Hendon, closure was inevitable. On 1st July 1903, Welsh Harp station was closed.

ONGAR

This terminus in the market town of Chipping Ongar, at the northernmost extremity of the Central line, opened in 1865 and operated right up until 1994. At the end of a single-track railway running from Epping (there was a passing point at North Weald station), it was famous for its scorpions, said to dwell in the sand laid to slow trains that overshot the stopping mark. Re-opened and operated by the Epping Ongar Railway Volunteer Rail Society between 2004 and 2007, the line was relaunched again – as the Epping Ongar Railway in 2012 – and now runs as a weekend service for tourists in summer. The name probably derives from the Saxon words *aungre* or *hangre* meaning place or hill. Chipping, like Cheapside, comes from Old English *cēping*, a market or market-place.

LORD'S

For a few months in the summer of 1939, the Middlesex Cricket Club managed to persuade the directors of the Metropolitan & St John's Wood Railway to change the name of St John's Wood station to Lord's Station. The station was renamed on 11th June 1939, just five months before the station closed as a result of services transferring to the new deep-level tunnels between Finchley Road and Baker Street (for the Bakerloo line). The remains of Lord's Station are now under the Danubius Hotel in Regent's Park; cricket fans carrying hampers and booze like to chant for the reopening of the station. St John's Wood, twice as far away from the cricket ground, has been part of the Jubilee Line since 1979. In an interesting suburban sidenote, blueprint Tube maps from 1938–9 indicate that St John's Wood station was originally to be given the name Acacia Road or Acacia.

THE FLEET LINE

In the mid 1960s the government considered a scheme to open a line that would run from Baker Street to Bond Street and Trafalgar Square and then go east along the Strand and Fleet Street to Cannon Street, before proceeding into south-east London. The line would follow the Tyburn stream for much of its central London route and pass under the River Fleet – London's largest subterranean river – at Ludgate Circus. Construction began in 1971 but by the time the work was completed in 1979, the line had only reached Charing Cross (with new plans to extend the route on the opposite bank of the Thames) and the name had been changed to Jubilee to celebrate the Queen's 25 years on the throne in 1977. The original choice of battleship grey for the line's colour was based on the naval meaning of the word "fleet"; this became a lighter grey, to suggest the silver colour of the Jubilee.

I want to go back to London

I want to go back to London town
To ride once more in a motor bus
Or a tuppenny tube go down
I want to go back to London
I don't care how slow the train
When to town I come, I will make things hum
For I mean to see life again

From a popular song (1912)

A God for London?

Over two years passed, and the Schlegel household continued to lead its life of cultured, but not ignoble, ease, still swimming gracefully on the grey tides of London. Concerts and plays swept past them, money had been spent and renewed, reputations won and lost, and the city herself, emblematic of their lives, rose and fell in a continual flux, while her shallows washed more widely against the hills of Surrey and over the fields of Hertfordshire. This famous building had arisen, that was doomed. To-day Whitehall had been transformed; it would be the turn of Regent Street to-morrow. And month by month the roads smelt more strongly of petrol, and were more difficult to cross, and human beings heard each other speak with greater difficulty, breathed less of the air, and saw less of the sky. Nature withdrew; the leaves were falling by midsummer; the sun shone through dirt with an admired obscurity.

To speak against London is no longer fashionable. The Earth as an artistic cult has had its day, and the literature of the near future will probably ignore the country and seek inspiration from the town. One can understand the reaction. Of Pan and the elemental forces, the public has heard a little too much – they seem Victorian, while London is Georgian – and those who care for the earth with sincerity may wait long ere the pendulum swings back to her again. Certainly London fascinates. One visualises it as a tract of quivering grey, intelligent without purpose, and excitable without love; as a spirit that has altered before it can be chronicled; as a heart that certainly beats, but with no pulsation of humanity. It lies beyond everything; Nature, with all her cruelty, comes nearer to us than do these crowds of men. A friend explains himself; the earth is explicable – from her we came, and we must return to her. But who can explain Westminster Bridge Road or Liverpool Street in the morning – the city inhaling – or the same thoroughfares in the evening – the city exhaling her exhausted air? We reach in desperation beyond the fog, beyond the very stars, the voids of the universe are ransacked to justify the monster, and stamped with a human face. London is religion's opportunity – not the decorous religion of theologians, but anthropomorphic, crude. Yes, the continuous flow would be tolerable if a man of our own sort – not any one pompous or tearful – were caring for us up in the sky.

From Howard's End *(1910) by EM Forster*

Train tweet
National Rail @nationalrailenq

#Nuneaton – Ticket acceptance is no longer available on Chiltern Railways

MY COMMUTE: THE PSYCHOGEOGRAPHER

Laura Oldfield Ford, Whitechapel to Barking, 2010–the present

I walk from Commercial Road to Whitechapel High Street, drifting through dusty hospital corridors and fluorescent ranks of ambulances. The Royal London is a gated citadel with Victorian sections in a state of partial demolition and PFI towers gleaming in a thin grey sky. It is 8 in the morning and the station is a frenzied burrow, crushes of people heading westbound to office jobs in the centre or across the road to shifts in wards and laundries.

I am travelling the other way, against the tide. I board an almost empty eastbound District Line train and it feels luxurious to be heading out, away from the crowds.

The train edges through Stepney, a few passengers get on, mostly from Sylhet and Dhaka. At Mile End there is a little flurry as people step across the platform to the Central Line. An old man in salwar kameez disdainfully hurls a worn copy of the *Metro* aside and sits down. A construction worker in powdery overalls scrolls through texts.

There is space in the carriage. It is quiet. I look at my phone, write some emails and wait to get a signal.

We emerge suddenly in crystalline sunshine and glide through the new Barratt fortresses and council blocks of Bromley-by-Bow. This is a spectacular moment when the vistas of Canary Wharf, Canning Town and West Ham unfurl in a golden light that shocks me out of my dream state.

The train crosses the Bow Back Rivers, over footpaths that pull you irresistibly from Stratford to Limehouse Basin.

I look at the snarls of wilderness left over from the Olympic land grab, the abandoned office blocks and marshy tributaries of the Lea. This is the site of the proposed mega-mosque; the plans have been temporarily abandoned but the site is still charged, contested. Beyond the expanse of ragwort and gorse is the '80s Tesco that will form the heart of the planned "Tesco village" where schools, flats and doctors' surgeries will be subsumed under that ubiquitous logo.

I pass through these liminal zones every day. It's a strange area that I know in fragments, a difficult place to walk around. There are gas holders and isolated workers' cottages concealed behind canopies of elderflower, and traveller sites stranded between canals and train tracks. I think a lot about islands on my journeys through here, or really phantom islands, places that exist for a while and then just disappear so I'm never certain if I mistook them for somewhere else.

THE CITY GENT – STRIPPED

9. THE RAZOR

Naked – but not quite – for he holds
his Truefit and Hill faux ivory number,
an old Christmas gift from the long-
departed kids, and a Taylor's badger
brush bent by the years. Well lathered,
he has time – tomorrow's shave shall be
brisk and superficial – to work slowly,
carefully, taking pleasure in the sound
of the scything of every bristle. Your
dad always had to shave twice a day,
too. Even now readying himself for the
next day's commute, as much as for bed,
the novel, his wife, sleep. A cut-throat
stands, closed, in the seaside-blue
gel mug to the left. It dates from his
college days, but he can't remember if
he bought it or if it was a hand-down
from the old man. He used to love the
performance of using it, imagining he
was Brando in *Last Tango*. "A barber…
a madman". On the right, alongside her
white and pink executive shaver, is his
hardly-used multi-bladed modern affair;
every 10 years they add a new blade
to men's shavers, and that whitening
strip telling you when to change it.
They must think we're stupid. In the
Metro, that very morning, he'd read
that *Skyfall* had made the cut-throat
fashionable again. A 400 per cent
increase in sales. But Daniel Craig's no
Brando; he's not even the best James
Bond. The lather almost gone now,
and his face staring back at him. He
lowers his head and looks up – isn't that
what models are trained to do – and
then does the opposite, pushing his
jaw towards the mirror. From either

angle his eyes look baggy and his chin
doubled. There's a skin tag where his
collar rubs: *acrochordon*. He googled
it. Someone on the radio – a handsome
devil in his 50s – said a splash of cold
water tightens the skin, making it look
youthful. A handy tip for the morning,
but to look tight and young for bed? He
squeezes out some of the mint-scented
after-shave lotion and enjoys the sting.
Outside a fox, somewhere, screams. A
train goes past. Must be the last service:
the 12:20 through to Portsmouth. He
wonders, again, if that's the same one
that comes to collect him at 7:14. But
they're longer at night, bizarrely, and he
reminds himself to write a letter about
that, the four carriages, to someone
at Southwest. But he won't. He'd hate
to become the kind of old fart who
writes letters to the newspapers and
faceless corporations. Beyond the
tracks, that lie above the back garden
on an embankment built in the 1870s,
the cemetery. He hears his wife moving
around the bedroom. She'll want to do
her ablutions now. He blasts the razor
with the cold-water tap and sees the
hairs scatter around the bowl of the
sink. He remembers a poster of a man
arriving home in the 1950s, his hand on
the garden gate, his wife, in an evening
gown, at the door, the trees throwing
long, not exactly ghostly, shadows on
to the lawn, and the detail: the hand
wavering, not sure it wants to move the
gate and arrive, his own hand moves
towards the bathroom door handle…

"Baker St Station Buffet"

Smoothly from Harrow, passing Preston Road,

They saw the last green fields and misty sky,

At Neasden watched a workmen's train unload,

And, with the morning villas sliding by,

They felt so sure on their electric trip

That Youth and Progress were in partnership.

Extract, by John Betjeman (1954)

Life Expectancy and Child Poverty in London

Income Deprivation Affecting Children Index: darker shades are areas of
higher deprivation. Life Expectancy at birth for areas adjacent to Tube stations.

Bloodletting

Yet if the Underground system of arteries and veins in London created a more mixed city, this mixture had sharp limits in time. During the day, the human blood of the city flowed below ground into the heart; at night, these subterranean channels became veins emptying the mass out of the centre, as people took the Underground home. With mass transit on the model of the Underground, the time geography of the modern urban centre had now taken form: density and diversity by day, sparsity and homogeneity by night. And that mixture by day implicated no strong human contact between the classes. People worked and shopped and then left for home.

From Flesh and Stone: The Body and City in Western Civilisation, *by Richard Sennett (1994)*

The Getaway (Lonesome Train)

Every time I hear that lonesome train roll down the track
Going away to unknown destinations
I believe there's someone out there making the great escape
Just moving on, suddenly gone and so unexpectedly

It might hit you on a sunny afternoon
Without a warning there's a thought, it just comes over you
And is the shadow on a sidewalk someone like you?
In a blink of an eye, waving goodbye
It's time you made your getaway

In a suburb somewhere someone's quietly planning their getaway
Travelling light, in case they might get a change of heart
It's the bravest move they'll ever make, but they have to make the break
That's the risk that they take, so don't hesitate, then so unexpectedly

It might hit you on a sunny afternoon
Without a warning there's a thought, it just comes over you
And it's a shadow on the sidewalk, someone you knew
It's time you made your getaway

Ray Davies, from the album Other People's Lives *(2006)*

The romance of business

"It is the fashion nowadays," said Clovis, "to talk about the romance of Business. There isn't such a thing. The romance has all been the other way, with the idle apprentice, the truant, the run-away, the individual who couldn't be bothered with figures and book-keeping and left business to look after itself. I admit that a grocer's shop is one of the most romantic and thrilling things I have ever happened upon, but the romance and thrill are centred in the groceries, not the grocer. The citron and spices and nuts and dates, the barrelled anchovies and Dutch cheeses, the jars of caviar and chest of tea, they carry the mind away to Levantine coast towns and tropic shores, to the Old World wharfs and quays of the Low Countries, to dusty Astrachan and far Cathay; if the grocer's apprentice has any romance in him it is not a business education he gets behind the grocer's counter, it is a standing invitation to dream and to wander, and to remain poor. As a child such places as South America and Asia Minor were brought painstakingly under my notice, the names of their principal rivers and the heights of their chief mountain peaks were committed to my memory and I was earnestly enjoined to consider them as parts of the world that I lived in; it was only when I visited a large well-stocked grocer's shop that I realized that they certainly existed. Such galleries of romance and fascination are not bequeathed to us by the business man; he is only the dull custodian, who talks glibly of Spanish olives and Rangoon rice, a Spain that he has never known or wished to know, a Rangoon that he has never imagined or could imagine. It was the unledgered wanderer, the careless-hearted seafarer, the aimless outcast, who opened up new trade routes, tapped new markets, brought home samples or cargoes of new edibles and unknown condiments. It was they who brought the glamour and romance to the threshold of business life, where it was promptly reduced to pounds, shillings and pence; invoiced, double-entried, quoted, written off, and so forth; most of these terms are probably wrong, but a little inaccuracy sometimes serves tons of explanation.

"On the other side of the account there is the industrious apprentice, who grew up into the business man, married early and worked late, and lived, thousands and thousands of him, in little villas outside big towns. He is buried by the thousand in Kensal Green and other large cemeteries; any romance that was ever in him was buried prematurely in shop and warehouse and office. Whenever I feel in the least tempted to be business-like or methodical or even decently industrious I go to Kensal Green and look at the graves of those who died in business."

From "Clovis on the Alleged Romance of Business" from The Square Egg and Other Sketches *(1924) by Saki (HH Munro)*

And if a double-decker bus

"The Routemaster was a vehicle built in London, maintained in London and operated in London for over 50 years. A favourite not only with the operating staff, but also with passengers and the general public alike. Although a 1950s design, it was well ahead of its time and despite several attempts, no successor has ever been found, and the Routemaster is a survivor."
Andrew Morgan, Chairman of the Routemaster Association

Morrisey's much-hummed song about a couple whose love becomes eternal thanks to a speeding bus should one day be rewritten for a Routemaster enthusiast. One of a handful of British motor vehicles that inspire intense fondness (the E-type Jaguar, Land Rover Defender and original Mini belong to the same tiny club), the RM class red bus is also a deep, dreamy fount of nostalgia for its fans.

Developed by engineering firm AEC in Southall and its sister company Park Royal Vehicles, a prototype Routemaster was presented at the Earl's Court Commercial Motor Show in 1954 and the bus went into service on London's roads in 1956. Some 2,876 would eventually be built, replacing the capital's electric trolleybuses and ageing RT, RTL and Titan RW diesel buses.

The RM buses were front-engined with a hop-on, hop-off rear platform and a conductor. The former gave passengers autonomy – they could jump off at their precise destination – and the clack-ching of the ticket machine and the "Allo darling, that'll be threepence" aspect of the ride made the experience social. The buses had semi-automatic transmission and power steering, which made driving more pleasant, and supple suspension, which benefited all. Despite their lighter, aluminium construction, they could each carry 64 passengers – 8 more than the RT buses. They were also simple to maintain and cheap to run. A dream machine, in short, at least for their era.

The last Routemaster rolled off the production line in 1968. In 1970, London Transport declared: "By the end of the decade, every London Transport bus will be operated by one man." In fact the Routemaster survived until 2005 and there are still two heritage services: the No. 9 from Olympia to Trafalgar Square and the No. 15 from Trafalgar Square to Tower Hill. Nonetheless, you are more likely to come across one of these red beauties at a classic vehicle rally or being employed as a moving corporate banner.

"There is a certain quality about the Routemaster," says Andrew Morgan. "I have always called it a glorified Meccano kit that over the years can be rebuilt, re-engined, and restored numerous times with relative ease. When the buses left London service from the mid-1980s, they made new friends across the British Isles and can now be found in virtually all corners of not only this country but around the world."

In June 2013, the New Bus for London – sometimes nicknamed the new Routemaster – went into full operational service on the No. 24 route between Pimlico and Hampstead Heath. In 2014, the Routemaster celebrated its 60th anniversary.

THE ROUTEMASTER
Myth versus Health and Safety

FANS SAY	OPPONENTS SAY
Convenient	Dangerous
Cheery conductor	Superfluous paid passenger
Cosy and warm	Cramped and stinking
I can get off where I live	So can a fare-dodger
Characterful and honest	Noisy and dirty
Totally original	Same as an old RT bus
Timeless	Wheelchair-unfriendly
Vintage	Old
An icon	A bus

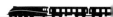

Commutourism
What will it be like in the post-commuter world?

In a hundred years time, if the futurists are proven correct, commuting will have gone the way of horses and carts. Tourists – enjoying a day away from their home workstation – will catch heritage commuter trains to London. This is what their guides will say, probably…

"Welcome on board 'commuters'!!! This is the 7:59 Milton Keynes to Euston semi-fast London Midland service, calling at Bletchley, Leighton Buzzard, Hemel Hempstead and Watford Junction. Standing room only. Move along the aisles to make room for fellow passengers. Don't lean on the doors. Don't put your feet up. Don't open a can of drink. Report any suspicious objects. Keep your own bags by your side at all times. Stand up to allow pregnant women or those with mobility challenges to take a seat. Some toilets are locked. The rest are blocked. No music, no alcohol, no food, no frotting, no joke…

Yes folks, that's the way it was back in the early twenty-first century. A 'commuter' was someone who had to be trafficked to and from work on a daily basis. Generally he logged on at a multi-floor building and complied with an office rota, which was tied to his monthly income. He made the trip to and from his remote workstation for many years, always at approximately the same time. Though the combined journeys could amount to up to three hours each day, the equivalent of more than four years in a working lifetime, he never protested. The twist was: the 'commuter' paid for all this out of his own funds.

Back then, getting to work was the biggest job of all. Close your eyes, just as the sleepy 'commuters' would do every morning, and imagine. The carriage was tropical, or Arctic, clammy and yet drafty. Hushed but somehow noisy. Germs, the records prove, travelled in greater comfort than the passengers.

Like my hat? It's a bowler I bought during a gap-week in Bolivia. The history books tell us that this is the helmet the commuter used to protect himself from the rain. On Sundays he carried deodoriser in an executive case. He also took along a sheet of printed newsfeed, an apple and an ancient Biro ink-pen.

Time was everything to the 'commuter'. He wore a watch, there were clocks all over the place, complicated timetables were drawn up for the train – and yet he never managed to arrive anywhere on time.

We will though – and we'll be pulling away from the stand – sorry, I should say 'platform' – at noon.

These screens on your left and right are windows. Digigraphs show that most 'commuters' omitted to observe the scenescapes that scrolled past the window. But do look through the glass from time to time as it's the view that tells the story. Take our origin, MK SuperCity, built in the 1970s as one of the late-phase Garden-City project developments and retailed to inner-capitalists as 'good for your health'. Concrete cows were planted in patches of fallow and in 1982 this station was opened to slot the new town into the shunting track known as the West Coast Mainline. As you can see, the station sits in a tree-less megaplaza. MK was given a good weeding and the Garden bit got buried under smooth ConcPlast. Thank Goodness.

Right, it's noon, I'm getting the signal in my Moby that we're off. Hold tight, we'll be going at maximum commuter speed: 40 miles per hour. In yottabyte per second terms that's like waiting for a 10-second video to download for, like, a decade. Enjoy the ride…

My analogue map says there used to be woodlands visible through the window here. Organically sourced ash dieback and the nationwide fracking boom – boom being the operative word after Blackpool fell into the grand Fylde canyon – put paid to that, and now we only have these awesome storage units, logistics bastions and eco-cess pit energy banks.

We're stopping symbolically at Bletchley. No one got on or off anything here in more than 30 years. Believe it or not, this was once a strategic collection point for 'commuters'. It was also a thought-laboratory during the second twentieth century war. At an old mansion known as Station X a primitive code called Enigma was broken. The town lived off this for as long as it could, but MK eventually absorbed Bletchley and gave it the civic upgrade it desperately needed.

See all the traffic on the left? We're running parallel to the Grand Union Throughway for much of this journey. In the early twenty-first century the GU was a canal, an artificial river full of stagnant water and water-gates which the 'commuters' liked to float up and down on at the weekends using boats that were slower than an iPhone24.

Leighton Buzzard is named after a large carrion-eating raptor that went extinct in 2047. In Q4 of the twentieth century, an eponymous musical group had a hit download with a track called 'Saturday Night Beneath the Plastic Palm Trees'. This was known as a 'new' wave song and proved prophetic, as many high-earning residents of Bedfordshire – the quaint old county to which this Buzzard belonged – did indeed go off on holidays to fabricated resort towns in Ye Olde Dubai.

The next section was fields and cows and badgers and tuberculosis until about 80 years ago. Now it's the Cameron-Osborne Estate, 500 acres of quasi-affordable micro housing for the bean-counters who do the night shifts for India's cyberRed. And here's some local news! Last week a bra-making bootleg sweatshop in Tring – named after the bells trains once rang when they refused to stop here - was closed down.

Don't blink, that was Berkhamsted.

We're just into the Tube zone now. The HS2 and HS3 lines meet west of here, carrying shuttles to the Virgin H-Row Hub. The CrossNorth Tube transit starts at Bushey, going subsurface at Barnet and surfacing at Gatwick Hub. See the old Borisken? Yep, more tourists, on our Backender tour? £95, map included.

Ah, Hemel Hempstead. This metropolitan banlieue was, with Tunbridge Wells, Surbiton, High Wycombe and Bishop's Stortford, one of the archetypal 'commuter towns'. If someone said 'I'm from Hemel', everybody knew what he meant. What he meant was: 'I am law-abiding, I am respectable, I have two children, a spouse and a pedigree dog, I am a home-owner, I am hard-working, I pay tax; I can afford one

foreign holiday a year; I like to think of myself as broad-minded; I have aspirations; People think I am a cipher but I am an individual; I have inner depths that the world never dreams of…'

Now Hemel is a sink city for prison officers, maids and veg merchants.

Watford was once the hypothetical upper border of the Sahfeest – before the Big Wall was erected. It was a popular 'dormitory town', a place for employees to go to sleep after their train journeys home. 'North of Watford' signified 'zone of barbarians', much as 'Beyond Shakeytown' does nowadays. Now Watford is a craft-and-latte nexus for the upper-lower-median classes.

What you can see now is not so different from what our ancestors saw: the Great North Circular Hyper-ring, though back then it didn't have 40 lanes; the Harrow SuperAcademy; the Tesco & Spencers ExtraMalls; the grey sky; and a million little cars and a million little houses. Nice to know some things never change.

We'll be getting off just beyond the Betjeman Stadium to jump on steam-powered Segskates. That'll be a relief I'm sure, but as you know, trains aren't allowed in to the Lundenwic finance zone any more than 'commuters' these days. Homework equals leisure equals wonderful daytrips like this.

The terminal here, Ex-Euston, is a theatre set that replicates the original. Look out for the Doric arch, the actors pretending to be waiting angrily and the low-flying pigeons. I hope you enjoyed your 'commute'. The doors will open shortly. Mind the gap between the train and the platform edge."

Charon

The conductor's hands were black with money:

Hold on to your ticket, he said, the inspector's

Mind is black with suspicion, and hold on to

That dissolving map. We moved through London,

We could see the pigeons through the glass but failed

To hear their rumours of wars, we could see

The lost dog barking but never knew

That his bark was as shrill as a cock crowing,

We just jogged on, at each request

Stop there was a crowd of aggressively vacant

Faces, we just jogged on, eternity

Gave itself airs in revolving lights

And then we came to the Thames and all

The bridges were down, the further shore

Was lost in fog, so we asked the conductor

What we should do. He said: Take the ferry

Faute de mieux. We flicked the flashlight

And there was the ferryman just as Virgil

And Dante had seen him. He looked at us coldly

And his eyes were dead and his hands on the oar

Were black with obols and varicose veins

Marbled his calves and he said to us coldly:

If you want to die you will have to pay for it.

Louis MacNeice (1962)

Wartime window view

A noisy night, L. only woken once but he was very late in going to sleep. I age inwardly when the war disturbs him, it's so unfair. We got up a bit earlier than usual and I rang the railway to see if trains were normal, then caught one at 8.20 to town. By tube to Paddington for Reading, found the station rather forlorn but crowded owing to a serious upset near Ealing. There was an occasional main line train but no time-table at all. I had a travel voucher to Reading, rang the S.R. and found there was an alternative route. After 35 minutes the G.W.R. suggested that Reading passengers should go to Oxford on the way, this seemed to me absurd so I went to Waterloo and got an electric train to Reading. The damage to houses near the line of the S.R. in London was very serious in the first few miles. I travelled alone in a 1st class car and read a history of the Quakers, or alternately practised the recorder a bit, which I can do while looking out of the window.

Mass Observation, Saturday 16th November 1940 (Diarist 5216)

The galleries of the dead

We had entered an immense traffic jam. From the junction of the motorway and Western Avenue to the ascent ramp of the flyover the traffic lanes were packed with vehicles, windshields leaching out the molten colours of the sun setting above the western suburbs of London. Brake-lights flared in the evening air, glowing in the huge pool of cellulosed bodies. Vaughan sat with one arm out of the passenger window. He slapped the door impatiently, pounding the panel with his fist. To our right the high wall of a double-decker airline coach formed a cliff of faces. The passengers at the windows resembled rows of the dead looking down at us from the galleries of a columbarium. The enormous energy of the twentieth century, enough to drive the planet into a new orbit around a happier star, was being expended to maintain this immense motionless pause.

From Crash *(1973) by JG Ballard*

Take me home

And then the spaces between towns began to widen. The road sliced unsentimentally through flat fields. There was nothing there, nothing to see, only the night rushing towards the coach's windscreen, and the shrinking tail-lights of overtaking cars.
From Divided Kingdom *(2005) by Rupert Thomson*

Commuter's hands: a preliminary study

We were surprised by the very high rates of detection of bacteria of faecal origin on hands. Though the presence of such bacteria is probably not a health hazard in itself, it is indicative of a failure of hygiene, and more specifically a failure to wash hands after contact with faecal material or surfaces where faecal material is present. We were also surprised to note the clear and significant geographic trend with lower isolation rates in Southern cities gradually rising to higher rates the further north the samples were taken. This trend was due largely to a significant increase in detection of faecal bacteria on the hands of males, but not females, with increasing latitude. We can see no obvious reason for this. Commuters in some cities may have had longer journeys from home, and hence had longer for bacteria to die off. Sampling was carried out by different individuals in some cases on different days and may have been less thorough in some cites than others, and train and bus cleaning regimes may have varied from city to city. Climatic conditions may also have varied. However, there is no reason to expect that any of these factors would have varied in a systematic way in males so as to produce the pattern observed. We therefore propose further investigation of the hypothesis that hands are washed more often or more thoroughly in the South of the UK relative to the North, and that male and female handwashing rates differ geographically.
From "Isolation of bacteria of faecal origin on commuters' hands: a preliminary study" by Gaby Judah, Peter Donachie, Emma Cobb, Mark Holland and Val Curtis

Train tweet
29th January: Leonie Pitts @leonieash

Train delayed and a girl's sneeze LANDED on my hand!!!!!!
Can't wait to rid myself of this commute!! #London

Nothing

Perhaps the wisest commuters are, after all, those who see nothing, learn nothing, know nothing. They have no delusions. They resemble those sailors who refuse to master the art of swimming so that they may drown quickly and painlessly if their ship sinks.

From Notes from Overground *(1984) by Tiresias (aka Roger Green)*

Shhh

SHAKESPEARE...
Weary with toil, I haste me to my bed,
The dear repose for limbs with travel tired;
But then begins a journey in my head...
Sonnet 27

Rosaline:
How many weary steps,
Of many weary miles you have o'ergone,
Are number'd in the travel of one mile?
Love's Labour's Lost, V:2

Claudio:
O, what men dare do! What men may do! What men daily
Do, not knowing what they do!
Much Ado About Nothing, IV:1

... AND SHEENA
My baby takes the morning train
He works from nine til five and then
He takes another home again
To find me waiting for him.

In my end is my beginning

INDEX

Photographs in **bold**

FURTHER READING

Ackroyd, Peter *London: A Biography* (Chatto & Windus 2000)

Austen, Jane *Sense and Sensibility* (Thomas Egerton, 1811)

Ballard JG *Crash* (Cape, 1973)

Barker, Paul *The Freedoms of Suburbia* (Frances Lincoln, 2009)

Barnes, Julian *Metroland* (Cape, 1980)

Beaumont, Matthew and Dart, Gregory eds. *Restless Cities* (Verso, 2010)

Beckett, Samuel *Waiting for Godot* (Faber & Faber, 1956)

Betjeman, John *A Few Late Chrysanthemums* (John Murray, 1954)

Blake, William *The Complete Poetry and Prose* Edited by David V Erdman (Anchor, 1988)

Cobb, Richard *Still Life* (Chatto & Windus / Hogarth Press, 1983)

Cunningham, Gail and Barber, Stephen *London Eyes: Reflections in Text and Image* (Berghahn, 2007)

Davis Michael, Jennifer *Blake and the City* (Bucknell University Press, 2007)

De Botton, Alain *The Pleasures and Sorrows of Work* (Hamish Hamilton, 2009)

Eliot, TS *The Four Quartets* (Harcourt, 1943); *The Waste Land* (Horace Liveright, 1922)

Engels, Friedrich *The Condition of the Working Class in England* trans. Florence Kelley Wischnewetzky (Swan Sonnenschein & Co, 1892)

Forster, EM *Howard's End* (Edward Arnold, 1910)

Grossmith, George and Weedon *Diary of a Nobody*
(JW Arrowsmith, 1892)

Hamilton, Patrick *Slaves of Solitude* (Constable, 1947)

Heidegger, Martin *Being and Time* trans. Joan Stambaugh
(State University of New York, 2010); *Country Path Conversations*
trans. Bret W Davis (Indiana University Press, 2010)

Howard, Ebenezer *Garden Cities of Tomorrow*
(Swan Sonnenschein & Co. Ltd., 1902)

Idzikowsi, Chris *Sound Asleep: The Expert Guide to Sleeping Well* (Watkins, 2013)

Kierkegaard, Søren *Repetition: A Venture in Experimental Psychology*
trans. Walter Lowrie (Princeton University Press, 1941)

Lanchester, John *Mr Phillips* (Faber, 2000); *What We Talk About When We Talk
About The Tube: The District Line* (Particular Books, 2013)

Mabey, Richard *A Good Parcel of English Soil: The Metropolitan Line*
(Particular Books, 2013)

Nietzsche, Friedrich *On the Genealogy of Morals* trans. William A Hausemann
(Macmillan, 1897)

Self, Will *The Book of Dave* (Viking, 2006)

Sennett, Richard *Flesh and Stone: The Body and City in Western Civilisation*
(WW Norton & Co, 1994)

Sinclair, Iain *London Orbital* (Granta, 2003)

Thomas, Leslie *Tropic of Ruislip* (Eyre Methuen, 1974)

Tiresias (aka Green, Roger) *Notes from Overground* (Paladin, 1984)

Wragg, David *Commuter City: How the Railways Shaped London*
(Wharncliffe Books, 2010)

ACKNOWLEDGEMENTS

Thanks to Annabel Barber and Blue Guides, and to Pete Fiennes for supporting the project. TJ Brooke Bullard, Elli Christie and Theo Gordon were invaluable researchers and all my confessors would be great company on a commute. Bob Greig talked train trivia and Kate Miller talked sense. A wave to Southern trains for not being corporate all the time. For disparate advice, thanks to Gail Cunningham, Pete Watts, Stephen Hayward and Simon Abernethy, and to the RSPB and Trees for Cities for their contributions and for rescuing our urbs, suburbs and exurbs. Thanks to the London Transport Museum and Museum of London for assistance with research and access to their fabulous archives. Thank you Stephen Reid for all your design work and for the little Mallard.

ed Poems by Frances Cornford (London: Enitharmon Press, 1996), reproduced with permission; Tony Hancock's "The Rebel" (1961), written by Ray Galton and Alan Simpson, reproduced by permission of STUDIOCANAL Films Ltd; Diary extract from Mass Observation courtesy of Trustees of the Mass Observation Archive, University of Sussex and Adam Matthews Digital/Sage; Dorothy Harris extract quoted in Humphries, Steve and Taylor, John *The Making of Modern London* Vol. 4 1945–85 (London: Sidgwick and Jackson, 1986); Tweets reproduced by permission; Ezra Pound's "In a Station of the Metro" reproduced by permission of Faber & Faber Ltd; Extracts from *Malone Dies* and *Proust* by Samuel Beckett reproduced by permission of Faber & Faber Ltd; Extract from AA Brill's translation of Freud reproduced courtesy of bartleby.com, Inc.; "Commuter" © 1981 by EB White, used by permission, all rights reserved; Extract from *Flesh and Stone: The Body and City in Western Civilisation* by Richard Sennett (1994) reproduced by permission of the author; Extract from *Still Life: Sketches from a Tunbridge Wells Childhood* by Richard Cobb (1983) reproduced courtesy of the Random House Group Ltd.

Images courtesy of the following sources:

HM Bateman Designs (© www.hmbateman.com) p. 103

Camilla Charnock (www.camillacharnock.com) p. 19, p. 39, p. 74, p. 151, p. 199

Dr. James Cheshire (www.mappinglondon.co.uk) pp. 216–7

Environmental Images/Universal Images Group/Science and Society Picture Library p. 227

Esme Fiennes pp. 176–7

Peter Fiennes p. 156

Garden Cities of Tomorrow *by Ebenezer Howard* (Swan Sonnenschein & Co. Ltd., 1902) p. 77

istockphoto.com: ©bergamont p. 96; ©chiarito p. 79; ©higyou p. 18; ©IVV79 p. 52; ©lepas2004 p. 79; ©Lusoimages p. 79; ©thumb p. 79; ©Tony_Kwan p. 122

Simon Key (www.keyart.co.uk) first appeared in *Private Eye*, p. 221

Hadley Kincade p. 59

Lock & Co p. 24

London Transport Museum Collection (© TfL) cover image, p. 5, p. 10, p. 40, p. 89, p. 153, p. 154, p. 160, p. 163, p. 165, p. 180, p. 194

The Lordprice Collection p. 63, p. 75, p. 99

Manchester Daily Express/Science and Society Picture Library p. 192, p. 202

Chris Moss pp. 28–9, p. 84, p. 104, p. 113, p. 115, p. 169, p. 175, p. 189

Museum of London p. 25, p. 34, p. 44, p. 67, p. 100, p. 108, p. 130, p. 132, p. 136, p. 144, p. 157, p. 185

National Railway Museum/Science and Society Picture Library p. 17, p. 22, p. 124, p. 143, p. 209

National Media Museum/Science and Society Picture Library p. 49

Laura Oldfield Ford p. 213

Pauk p. 47

Pushkin Museum p. 31

RSPB p. 171

Scotsman Publications Library p. 21

UIG History/Science and Society Picture Library p. 224

Wikipedia: *Metro-land and Extension Lines*, Metropolitan Railway, 1924, p. 66; photo by Robert Knapp p. 148; photo by Piccolo Namek p. 196

Wolf & Badger (wolfandbadger.com), polka dot tie, by permission p. 46